FAMOUS ADIRONDACK RESTAURANTS AND RECIPES

BY SUE SCHILDGE

SCHILDGE PUBLISHING COMPANY
Plattsburgh • Minneapolis • Burlington

First Edition, 1984
Second Printing, 1985
Revised Printing, 1986
Revised Printing, 1988

FOR ADDITIONAL COPIES, THERE ARE ORDER FORMS IN
THE BACK OF THE BOOK OR WRITE DIRECTLY TO:

Schildge Publishing Company
P.O. Box 1516
Plattsburgh, New York 12901

PUBLISHER: Sue Schildge
TEXT BY: Sue Schildge
EDITED BY: Lynda Bouyea
ARTIST: Ray LaMonda
CONSULTANT: Blanche Ford
TYPESETTING: Cecilia Garrow
LAYOUT: Crystal Roe

Printed in United States of America
By
NORTHEAST PRINTING COMPANY
63 Bridge Street
Plattsburgh, New York

TABLE OF CONTENTS

My sincere thanks to all of the restaurant owners, managers and chefs featured in this book for sharing their favorite recipes with me. Without them, this book would not have been possible.

It is with sincere appreciation that I acknowledge the businesses who have helped make possible this book about the Adirondacks and Champlain Valley. Their interest in the area will contribute to the future enjoyment of the region by both residents and visitors alike.

The business sponsors include Coldwell Banker Real Estate, The Alpine Cellar Restaurant, The Balsam House, The Bark Eater Lodge, Casa Del Sol Restaurant, The Charcoal Pit, Deer's Head Inn, Elm Tree Inn, Frederick's, The Juniper Boat Tours, Mirror Lake Inn, The Norm Foote Realtors, Paul W. Calkins Agency, The Red Fox Restaurant, The Royal Savage Inn, Valcour Lodge, Westport Yacht Club and The Whiteface Chalet.

INTRODUCTION

My idea for FAMOUS ADIRONDACK RESTAURANTS & RECIPES began when someone once approached me with the comment, "You'd go anywhere for a delicious meal wouldn't you?" My answer was obviously "yes, I enjoy good food." Finding restaurants with a comparable atmosphere is also a part of the experience of dining out.

Traveling on the Northway, you can easily miss the best part of the Adirondacks. Experiencing the historical heritage, traditions and excellent quality meals in an atmosphere best known to the area is the heart of this book.

The basic premise for restaurants to be included in the book was good food in places with lots of charm. As the book progressed so did the information to include histories of the areas and the restaurants and their owners.

This resulted in the collecting of recipes, recipes that are probably some of the best in the Adirondacks. Directions to help tourists and travelers find their way with suggestions of sightseeing, events and sports in the communities near the restaurants end each chapter.

For each restaurant included in the book, there are many others which could have been selected if time and space would have allowed. My choices are based on living in the area for a number of years and recommendations from travelers, sales people, the restaurant owners, friends--all the people who might spend time away from home but still in the Adirondack area.

The Adirondacks have been blessed with many experienced chefs, combined with those born and raised in the area with natural cooking talent. This combination in the wide variety of their excellent restaurants offers you a food tour, the most enjoyable way to experience the Adirondacks. None of the restaurants included require a dress code. They will offer you and your family a friendly welcome and invite you to taste their tempting cuisine. If one of the recipes that you read about in the book is not on the menu when you visit, it may have been replaced for one they thought you may enjoy more.

As you take your own personal dining tour of the Adirondacks, travel at your own pace, spend more time where you want to spend time. You'll experience mirror lakes, indescribable landscapes of mountains and sunsets, white waters and placid streams scented by acres of forest woods. The geography and scenery are matched only by the magnificent cuisine. It's all there for you to discover!

Add to this a climate of simplicity which produces your stay to be as active or as leisurely as best suits your style. Let your senses taste the heritage and music of this splendid mountain area. Top it off with the pleasure of meeting and talking with the charming people who live in this country comfort...and there you have it, the most irresistable eating experience in the spirit and splendor of the Adirondacks.

NOTES FROM OUR KITCHEN

FAMOUS ADIRONDACK Restaurants & Recipes offers you a whole world of cooking and dining experiences.

My hope is that you use these recipes with complete confidence, but be adventurous too! Follow your own tastes as some of these recipes may be quite different from your usual bill of fare.

Some of the recipes have been reduced to portions less than what the restaurants normally use to make it convenient for home cooking and baking.

Each recipe has been kindly collected and tested to insure you the greatest success. The most important ingredient used to insure the high standard of fine food is freshness of the products, from the first tender slice of onion to the healthiest cut of meat and freshest piece of fish. This we highly recommend to insure the high quality of eating that you are looking for.

All of the ingredients can be found at the local markets, supermarkets and gourmet shops. We have also prompted substitutes for your convenience in shopping and suggestions to guide you to your own needs in your home.

Happy Cooking Adirondack Style!

DEDICATION

To Mary Lee, my sister, who has seasoned my life by offering freely her food for thought. Also, to my father, my friend, and to the "Adirondackers" who recognize that this beautiful area gives nourishment time and time again.

FAMOUS ADIRONDACK RESTAURANTS & RECIPES introduces you to the best most delicious dining in the Adirondack-Lake Champlain region.

By taking your own tour as I have through the area, you will taste many recipes offered by each restaurant as their statement of culinary expertise.

By preparing these fine recipes in your home serving them to your family and friends, you can create a pleasant sense of appreciation and accomplishment.

The restaurants included in FAMOUS ADIRONDACK RESTAURANTS & RECIPES were chosen, not only for their recipe preparation, but also, for the important part that they play in our lives. Today, sharing our favorite restaurant with others answers our needs, for the inviting warmth and relaxed atmosphere are an important part of the age old ritual of dining out. Dining out is a celebration!

You, too, can capture this special spirit; eating and drinking together fosters comradeship and creates an experience that never existed before. From ancient times to today, the table is where the life and spirit are and the quality of food is its pleasure.

Whether dining in your home, or in one of these prominent restaurants, I know you'll enjoy FAMOUS ADIRONDACK RESTAURANTS & RECIPES.

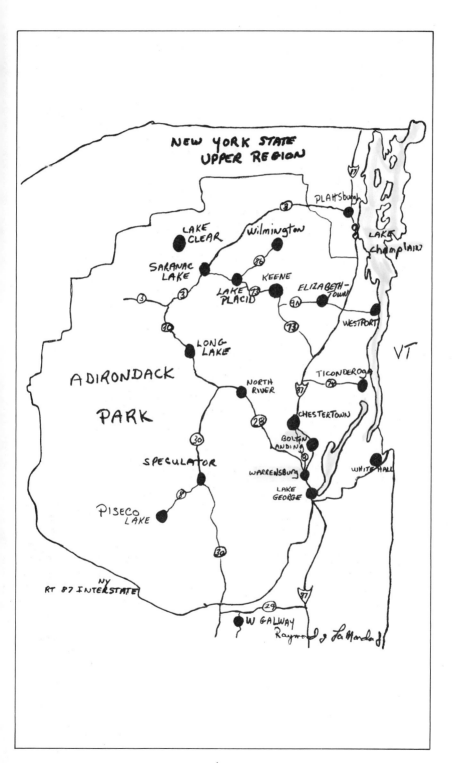

NEW YORK STATE
UPPER REGION

ADIRONDACK

PARK

NY
RT 87 INTERSTATE

ANTHONY'S

Just as exploration led Samuel de Champlain through the new waters of Lake Champlain in 1609, the same spirit of discovery, today, led Drew Sabella to open Anthony's Restaurant in 1980. Neither man was seeking land, power, fame or fortune, but only to explore an area unknown to most. Both men have similar qualities. Champlain had an adventurous spirit, a searching mind and an eye for new sights. Sabella, too, has an adventurous spirit, searching mind, a taste for superb food and a discerning eye for graceful decorating.

The restaurant, set in a remodeled 19th century farmhouse, features paintings by local artists which reflect the flickering candlelight, softly illuminating the large sunken dining room. Relaxed, semi-classical music and tantalizing aromas fill the air. Your evening can begin at a relaxed pace in the warm, cozy cocktail lounge.

Anthony's features an extensive nightly menu with twenty one different entrees. Your choices include: aged meats (cut to order) and fresh fish delivered from the New England coast four times weekly. The chef's list of innovative specialties rival the finest restaurants anywhere. Some of the creatively developed dishes are as follows; Veal Honfleuroise (thin slices of prime milk fed veal topped with shrimp), scallops and crabmeat in a cognac and cream sauce, twin fillets of beef stuffed with fresh oysters in a port wine/black peppercorn sauce or appetizers such as; escargot and scallops on a skewer wrapped with proscuitto ham served on a bed of fettuccini noodles with bernaise sauce.

Nearly everything is made from scratch in their kitchens, including the bread and desserts. A special way to conclude an evening at Anthony's; Chocolate Mousse Cake, Black Forest Cake, European style cheesecake or their own homemade ice creams.

Premier food, delightful atmosphere and a staff of caring professionals are the impressions left after a great evening at Anthony's. Whether you want a leisurely five course gourmet meal or a quick steak, Anthony's will accommodate you graciously.

Anthony's Drew Sabella has explored and discovered new dishes prepared in ways even your hopeful imagination never dreamed of, just as Samuel de Champlain explored and discovered the awesome beauty of Lake Champlain. Enjoy Anthony's as a part of the history of Plattsburgh and a part of Lake Champlain's heritage of excellent cuisine.

How to get there: *Off Exit 37 of I-87, turn left onto Rt. 3. Drive about 500 yards, Anthony's is on the right. Summer lunches. Dinner. Lounge. (518) 561-6420.*

While you're there: *The Plattsburgh area offers 2 beaches on Lake Champlain with camping. Near the Plattsburgh beach is the Aqua Park. It offers water slides, bumper boats, a concession stand, picnic facilities, changing rooms and showers.*
Flea markets. Shopping. Golf. Museums. Tennis. Boat Tour and aqua sports at Dock St. Lake Champlain is one of the best lakes for fishing. Perch, bass, pike, walleye, lake trout and salmon are plentiful.

VEAL DIJONAISE

1 oz. clarified butter
1/2 c. mushrooms, sliced
8-10 oz. of veal, cut into bite size chunks
1 t. shallots
6 oz. white wine
4 artichoke hearts, quartered
1-1/2 T. Dijon mustard
8 oz. heavy cream
Flour

1. Clarify butter by heating over very low heat to separate clarified oil from milk solids.
2. Simmer mushrooms in covered pan with 2 tablespoons of water for 5 minutes.
3. Add clarified butter to large hot saute pan.
4. Lightly flour veal and place in pan on high heat turning to brown lightly on all sides.
5. Add shallots, then wine, artichoke hearts, mustard, mushrooms (without liquid) and a twist of fresh black pepper.
6. Reduce (for two minutes) on high heat scraping drippings from pan.
7. Add cream. Simmer until cream begins to thicken. Add pinch of salt and serve.

NOTE: Boned chicken or turkey breast meat may be substituted for veal.

Serves: 2
Preparation: 30 minutes

SHRIMP FRANGELICO

1 oz. clarified butter
1 lb. shrimp, peeled and deveined
1 t. garlic, chopped
1 t. shallots, chopped
1 oz. Frangelico liquor
1/2 c. white wine
1 t. lemon juice
10-15 hazelnuts, chopped coarsely
1 T. butter
Chopped parsely
Toast points

1. Heat a large saute pan with 1 oz. clarified butter.
2. Lightly flour shrimp and place in hot pan. Saute on one side on medium heat until transparency is gone, then turn.
3. Add shallots, garlic, then one at a time Frangelico, lemon juice, white wine and a pinch of salt.
4. Simmer until shrimp are cooked through.
5. Sprinkle with chopped parsely and hazelnuts.
6. Whip in one tablespoon of butter until melted and serve on toast points.

NOTE: This is great as an appetizer for 4 or an entree for 2. Clarified butter: heat over low heat to separate clarified oil from milk solids.

Serves: 2
Preparation: 15 minutes

STRAWBERRY SORBET

1 qt. strawberries
2 c. plus 6 T. sugar
1 oz. white vinegar or lemon juice
2 c. white wine
3 egg whites
2 c. water

1. Place strawberries, two cups of sugar and vinegar in a saucepan and cook on medium heat stirring frequently until sugar is dissolved.
2. Puree in food processor or blender.
3. Add white wine and water.
4. Mix well and place in freezer until semi-frozen, approximately 3-8 hours.
5. Beat egg whites with 6 T. sugar until stiff.
6. Fold into semi-frozen mixture. Cover and allow to freeze overnight.

Serves: 12-15
Preparation: 20 minutes
Cooking: 8 minutes

CARBUR'S

PLATTSBURGH

Lunch or dinner at Carbur's follows a path so different from the other restaurants in Plattsburgh, it is difficult to explain what makes it so unusual.

Carbur's has discovered how to creatively assemble the sandwich into a culinary delicacy. Through a long term love affair with the sandwich, Carbur's concocts over one hundred superb sandwich combinations assembled especially for you with love, pride and imagination. A stickler for quality in its food and its appearance, a Carbur's sandwich is made from scratch with the best freshest ingredients available. Making a sandwich choice may stymie you, but it won't leave you hungry.

Carbur's Restaurant opened their doors for lunch and dinner in 1975. The restaurant features a twenty-five page "Eater's Digest" menu that lists over one hundred choice sandwiches, a page for vegetarians, fresh, crisp salad plates, scrumptious desserts, delicious "made from scratch" soups, and side orders with special sauce dips.

Carbur's offers fare as simple as a peanut butter sandwich to an incredible eighteen ounce boneless prime rib. Whatever you prefer, there is something about the selection and quality that you will find irresistible.

Carbur's welcomes you to a relaxed and friendly atmosphere. This lavish "old time" sandwich parlor has been decorated with many antiques, portraits, World War I recruiting posters, and stained glass lamps and windows. It is a place, whether you prefer dining privately or with a gathering of friends, where you may simply relax at your own pace in an authentic atmosphere.

At Carbur's, they are proud of "those unsung heroes in the kitchen lovingly, laboring over each creation--just for you."

How to get there: *124 Margaret St., Plattsburgh. Take Northway 87 to Route 3. Head east to downtown Plattsburgh. Turn right and you are there! (Across from the Clinton County Government Center). (518) 561-3663.*

While you're there: *The city beach is only 3 miles North on Route 9 (North Margaret St.) Cumberland Head Corners. Shopping within walking distance. Summer Theater. Golf. Tennis. Boat Tour. Boat rentals at the marinas. Ferry to Vermont. Magnificent scenery of Lake Champlain, one of the largest freshwater lakes in the United States.*

CHEESE SOUP

1 gallon milk
9 oz. Roux
3 T. sherry
2 T. worcestershire sauce
1 t. celery salt
1 t. white pepper
1/2 t. granulated garlic
2 lb. sharp cheddar cheese (grated)
1/2 lb. american cheese (grated)

1. Combine milk and roux in double boiler.
2. Whip together over medium heat.
3. As mixture thickens, add sherry, worcestershire, and seasonings.
4. When mixture reaches 130° add both cheeses, whipping well.
5. Stir frequently until cheeses are melted.
6. Cook one hour over low heat.
7. Strain through china cap (mesh strainer).
8. Cover immediately. Serve or refrigerate.

Serves: 12
Preparation: 1-1/2 hours

BACON DRESSING

2-1/2 lb. bacon
4-1/4 c. wine vinegar
1-3/4 c. lemon juice
1-1/4 c. sugar

1. Cut up and cook bacon in a pan.
2. Put sugar in a large mixing bowl.
3. Add wine vinegar and lemon juice. Mix until sugar is dissolved.
4. Add bacon after it has been rendered and cooked crisp.
5. Empty the bacon and fat into the bowl, but allow it to cool first.
6. Reheat when ready to serve.

NOTE: The dressing should be portioned so the entire amount need not be reheated every time.

Serves: 30
Makes 2 quarts
Preparation: 25 minutes

CAFE MOONEY BAY

POINT AU ROCHE

Lovely Point au Roche...situated on the shores of beautiful Lake Champlain, this resort and farm community presents a pleasant climate year around. Point au Roche offers scenic places to cool off, and it is a naturalist's paradise in summer. There is plenty of snow for cross-country in winter and first rate fishing in the spring and fall.

Overlooking Lake Champlain and pretty sailboats docked at the Mooney Bay Marina, you'll find Cafe Mooney Bay. It attracts diners to its friendly and casual charm to savor the culinary wizardry of Chef-Manager Kevin Everleth.

Chef Everleth speaks of his restaurant with pride and well he should! He is experienced and enthusiastic about his cuisine offered at the Cafe Mooney Bay. He is a graduate of the Culinary Institute at Hyde Park, New York and he perfected his knowledge of food working at the famous Barrows House in Dorset, Vermont until the summer of 1986 when he built and opened Cafe Mooney Bay offering sophisticated American food with the coveted French flair.

Large picture windows enable diners to enjoy the spectacular view of the sheltered Mooney Bay in this nautical, contemporary cafe. The color decor of the Mooney Bay restaurant consists of royal blue, yellow, and white as well as brass and a myriad of hanging plants which flatter the window-walled room overlooking Lake Champlain. Here in this delightful setting you can relax and enjoy some of the area's most delectable food preparations.

Once Chef Everleth is in his kitchen, the cuisine exalts his imagination and philosophy. Always he buys the freshest ingredients possible. He uses fresh herbs from his lovely herb garden growing right there on the premises. Eighty percent of the fresh fruits he uses are New York State grown and in season. He offers plenty of fresh fish such as tuna, salmon, red snapper, and bass. He is able to receive one day deliveries from Florida, New York City and Boston.

Appetizers include chilled peach and raspberry soup, Maine lobster bisque, and grilled quail with apples, watercress, and mustard sauce. Chef Everleth makes his crispy garden salads with seasonal greens and superior homemade dressings. As a purist, Chef Everleth offers a McIntosh apple and sweet basil sorbet to cleanse the palate prior to the enticing entree that you may choose such as braised rabbit with pimento and fresh herbs, prime calves' liver with proscuitto ham, port wine, and fresh sage, grilled sliced breast of duckling with raspberry sauce, or a New York sirloin with shiitake mushrooms in a light sauce. At times the everchanging menu may include venison, quail, pheasant, or Muscovy duck. No matter what is featured, the menu is continuously changing and is always a delightful lakeview feast with Chef Everleth at the helm.

Whether you're at Point au Roche for boating, or on the beach, or walking along a path, or taking a scenic drive for the beautiful views of Lake Champlain and Vermont, look for the large anchor at the restaurant's entrance. Here you can enjoy dinner well worth going out of your way again and again for finely-wrought cooking, beautiful relaxed surroundings, and attentive service. What a perfect way to end the day with cool breezes blowing and seagulls circling the bay and at a restaurant where you can enjoy an evening dinner prepared so caringly.

How to get there: *On Lake Champlain. Point au Roche is 5 miles north of Plattsburgh. Take Exit 40 of I-87 or follow Route 9 north of Plattsburgh and then turn right at the Point au Roche sign. Drive to Mooney Bay Marina. Cafe Mooney Bay is right there! It is about 10 minutes from Plattsburgh or about one hour's drive from Montreal. Dinner. Lounge. Outside deck. Banquets and wedding receptions. 518-563-3328.*

While you're there: *Fishing. Boating. Mooney Bay Marina with store, boat sales, docking facilities, laundromat, showers and winter boat storage. At Point au Roche there are cottages and a beautiful, newly-opened 860 acre Point au Roche State Park complete with beach, picnic ground, bathhouse, nature walks, and cross-country ski trails.*

CHILLED PEACH AND RASPBERRY SOUP

4 lbs. very ripe peaches
2½ lbs. red raspberries, cleaned
4-5 c. simple syrup
Juice of 2 lemons
2 c. white wine (or to your taste)
Whipped cream for garnish
Mint leaves for garnish

1. Cut the peaches in half and remove the seed and any pieces of the seed.
2. Puree the peaches as well as two pounds of the raspberries and the simple syrup.
3. Strain the mixture through a fine china cap to remove the seeds from the raspberries.
4. Add the lemon juice and white wine and mix thoroughly.
5. Adjust sweetness or tartness of soup to your liking.
6. To serve, place six or seven whole raspberries in a chilled soup cup or bowl. Garnish the soup with a dollop of whipped cream, a beautiful red raspberry and a set of mint leaves.

CHEF'S NOTE: Leftover soup may be frozen and used as a granite with a few adjustments.

Serves: 10-12
Preparation: 20 minutes

BRAISED RABBIT WITH PIMENTOS
AND FRESH CHIVES

1-2½-3 lb. rabbit
Salt and pepper
Flour for dredging
1 t. minced garlic
1 T. chopped shallots
1 c. rabbit stock (rib bones from rabbit, 4 oz. onion,
   2 oz. carrot, 2 oz. celery, 1 bouquet garni)
1½ c. white wine
½ c. heavy cream
1 T. pimento strips
1 T. fresh chive, chopped
3 T. olive oil
1 T. sweet butter

1. Cut the rabbit into 6 pieces, remove rib bones and reserve.
2. Season with salt and pepper. Dredge lightly with flour.
3. Roast the rib bones in a roasting pan until they are nearly golden brown. Add the carrots, onions, celery and carmelize well.
4. Place in a saucepot along with one cup of wine and two cups of water.
5. Simmer for one to two hours adding water as necessary to keep bones submerged. After two hours strain stock and reduce the liquid by one-half.
6. Sear the rabbit in the olive oil and remove from pan.
7. Add the garlic and shallots. Saute briefly until golden brown.
8. Deglaze with the white wine and rabbit stock. Add the rabbit and cook until the rabbit is fork tender approximately 10-15 minutes.
9. Remove the rabbit, reserve, keeping it warm. Add the heavy cream and reduce by one-half. Add the pimentos and chives and gently swirl in the whole butter.
10. Adjust seasonings to taste. Serve 1 hind, 1 front, 1 loin section for one person.
Serves: 2
Preparation: 45-60 minutes
Cooking time: 25 minutes

GRILLED PRIME VEAL CHOP WITH PORT WINE, PROSCUITTO AND FRESH SAGE

4 prime veal chops, cut from the rack and trussed to hold their shape. Remove string after searing.

Olive oil
Salt and pepper
1 T. shallots
1 c. port wine
4 oz. proscuitto ham, sliced thinly and julienned
1 T. fresh sage leaves, chopped
8 oz. demi glace or brown sauce *see glossary
¼ c. heavy cream (optional)
1 T. sweet butter
4 sage leaves, whole

1. Sear the veal chops briefly in a saute pan.
2. Remove from the pan and cover the bones with foil to prevent burning.
3. Place the chops on the grill for 5 minutes per side turning 90 degrees halfway through the cooking time on each side.
4. Add the shallots to the pan. Saute until they just turn golden and deglaze with the port wine being careful or the port wine will ignite over the open flame.
5. Add the demi glace, fresh sage and reduce by one-half.
6. If you chose add the cream, then the julienne proscuitto and finally swirl in the whole butter.
7. Adjust seasonings.
8. Place one veal chop per portion and spoon the sauce over the top.
9. Garnish with a beautiful leaf of fresh sage.

Serves: 4
Preparation: 25 minutes
Cooking: 10 minutes

M/V JUNIPER
On Beautiful Lake Champlain

THE JUNIPER
DINNER BOAT

PLATTSBURGH

A twin-diesel ferry boat cruises Lake Champlain near Plattsburgh every evening from May to October.

The Juniper, a sixty-five foot long tour boat, proudly features the finest aged sirloin steaks in the North Country.

For a delightful evening and a most exclusive dining experience, The Juniper is your "prime" choice.

The tour boat sails south from Plattsburgh around historic Valcour Island, along its tree lined coves and cliffs. Captain and owner, Frank Pabst, describes and brings to life his step by step account of Benedict Arnold's moves as commander of the first American fleet in the Battle of Valcour on October 11, 1776. He will describe many other lesser known treasure stories turning the enchanting atmosphere into a magical special occasion.

As the sun sets behind the majestic Adirondack Mountains, the Juniper anchors in a quiet cove. You can smell the heavenly steaks on the charcoal fire as you make your own creation at the salad bar. Seat yourself at your own captain's table set with fine china. Your steak will be cooked exactly to your taste and will remain one of the best that you have eaten for a long time.

On board after dinner, harmonizing music from the 40's and 50's invites "sing-a-longs" and dancing.

Frank's decor for dining is Lake Champlain! Large windows enable diners to view the beautiful lake, waterfronts and mountains. It is a view that goes on for miles, and, for years in your memory.

The Juniper has a comfortable, friendly atmosphere--much like the North Country. Its rustic waterfront informality all but guarantees that you'll meet new friends. In the unchartered wilderness course of Lake Champlain, it's refreshing to savor this little seamark of atmosphere and comradeship, while enjoying a great steak.

How to get there: *Foot of Dock St. Plattsburgh. Heritage Adventures, Inc. May-October. (518) 561-8970.*

While you're there: *In July an annual Sailboat race is held on Lake Champlain. Many lake artifacts can be seen at The Clinton County Historical Museum. Shopping. Beach. Boating. Fishing. Sail-boarding.*

BEEF BROCHETTE AU BURGUNDY

1 lb. sirloin, cubed (3/4")
Salt and pepper
Soy sauce
2 c. burgundy
2 bay leaves
1 t. peppercorns
Pinch of basil
Pinch of tarragon
6 garlic cloves, crushed
1/4 t. fresh ginger, diced
1/4 c. white vinegar

1. Blend the spices and liquids.
2. Add meat to marinade for 48 hours.
3. Skewer, charcoal and serve.

NOTE: This recipe makes an excellent meal in a crockpot. Cook on low for 5 hours. Add cornstarch to thicken gravy.

Serves: 4
Preparation: 5 minutes
Cooking: 10-15 minutes

THE JUNIPER

4 oz. orange juice
1 shot Yukon Jack Blend
1 shot Seagrams whiskey
1 splash of grenadine

1. Shake over ice, pour and enjoy!

Serves: 1
Preparation: 2 minutes

NOTES

THE TEQUINIE

3 oz. gin
1/2 oz. dry vermouth
1/2 oz. tequila

1. Serve over ice or up.

Serves: 1
Preparation: 2 minutes

NOTES

CAPTAIN'S DRESSING

8 oz. Regular Kraft french dressing
4 cloves of garlic, crushed
Pinch of tarragon

1. Blend together and let set for 24 hours.

Serves: 6-8
Preparation: 5 minutes

NOTES

THE GREEN MEANIE

1 shot of scotch
Splash of green Creme De Menthe

1. Mix over ice.

Serves: 1
Preparation: 2 minutes

NOTES

The
**ROYAL SAVAGE
INN**

THE ROYAL SAVAGE
OCT. 11, 1776

FLAGSHIP OF THE U.S. FLEET
ON LAKE CHAMPLAIN

ROYAL SAVAGE INN

PLATTSBURGH

Serving the North Country public for over fifty years, the Royal Savage Inn has become a mainstay in Plattsburgh's restaurant community. The Inn is named after the famous Revolutionary War flagship (Royal Savage) commanded by General Benedict Arnold. During the Battle of Valcour, October 11, 1776, the ship was grounded on Valcour Island. After the American colonists fled the hostile British fire, the battleship was set afire and settled on Lake Champlain's murky bottom.

The history of the Royal Savage Inn begins in 1776. Farmer WIlliam Guilliland, one of the first settlers in the North Country, owned a hay barn which today is the main lobby of the restaurant. In 1919, the barn, then owned by the Boothe family, was converted into a tea room. Marion Parkhurst leased it for several years naming it, "Better Ole."

In 1932, Newton and Marion Keith leased the building and later purchased it renaming it the Royal Savage Inn. The Keith family worked very hard for 38 years building their restaurant's reputation for delicious food, informal atmosphere and friendly and efficient staffing. They next added dining rooms, an antique shop and gift shop filled with many "take home" treasures.

Donald Benjamin and his wife Barbara, the present owners acquired the Inn in 1970. Don believes that the basic concept of running a restaurant is to make everyone feel comfortable. He later converted the antique shop into the "Spitfire Tavern," offering people a more relaxed atmosphere to enjoy their favorite pre-dinner cocktail. Another dining room, which overlooks the rambling Salmon River, was opened in 1974.

Fresh flowers grace each table. Entrees feature the finest, prime quality meats. The seafood is the freshest available and the desserts are homemade classic Americana. The rooms at the Royal Savage are tastefully decorated with interesting antiques and history momentos. There is a signed Wallace Nutting painting and an original Currier and Ives. The most unique antiques are the two large panes of Redford's Bulls Eye glass which were made in Redford, New York between 1834 and 1852.

Lunch or dinner at the Royal Savage is truly "Fine dining in an Early American Setting" with an added touch of good 'ole Yankee charm!

How to get there: The Inn is located on Route 9, (Lake Shore Road), 5 miles South of Plattsburgh-easy to find! Lunch. Dinner. Cocktail Lounge. Gift Shop. Open year round. (518) 561-5140.

While you're there: You are just 1 mile South of Bluff Point Golf Course, the third oldest course in United States. You can rent a canoe or practice your golf game at Day Brothers' Marine Shop, next to the golf course. AuSable Chasm is 9 miles south. It is a scenic, natural attraction offering both a walking tour and boat rides. A gift shop and restaurant are there for family fun. Camping nearby. Motels. Views of Lake Champlain along Route 9.

APRICOT "SMOOCH"

1 package butter cookies
3/4 c. butter
1 c. confectionary sugar
2 eggs
1/3 c. nuts, chopped
2 c. apricot jam
1 c. heavy cream, whipped

1. Roll cookies into crumbs.
2. Cover bottom of baked pie shell with one half crumbs.
3. Cream butter and sugar.
4. Add eggs, one at a time and beat well after each.
5. Spread mixture over crumbs.
6. Sprinkle with chopped nuts.
7. Top with Apricot jam.
8. Spread cream and sprinkle with remaining crumbs.
9. Chill thoroughly.

Serves: 8-10
Preparation: 15-20 minutes

APPLE BREAD

3/4 c. sugar
1/3 c. shortening
1-1/2 c. whole wheat flour
1/2 c. white flour
1 c. apples, ground with peel
2 eggs
1/2 t. salt
1 t. baking powder
1 t. soda
2 T. sour milk
1/2 c. nut meats, chopped

1. Cream shortening and sugar. Add eggs and beat.
2. Add apples, sour milk and soda.
3. Sift flour, salt and baking powder.
4. Mix with the whole wheat flour and nut meats. Stir together.
5. Bake in a.greased loaf pan 40 minutes at 350° oven.

Serves: 8-10
Preparation: 15 minutes
Cooking: 40 minutes

ROYAL SAVAGE SPECIAL RASPBERRY TART

4 c. flour
2-1/2 c. unblanched almonds, ground
1 t. cinnamon
1 t. baking powder
1 egg, slightly beaten
2 c. sugar
2 c. butter
1/4 t. cloves
4 c. thick raspberry jam

1. Sift flour, sugar, baking powder, cinnamon, cloves in a large mixing bowl.
2. Add almonds which have been ground with the finest blade.
3. Cut in butter with hands until it resembles meal.
4. Add lightly beaten egg and knead until the mixture forms a soft ball.
5. Press two-thirds of the mixture into pan, 10"x16" cooking sheet.
6. Spread with raspberry jam.
7. Roll out remaining dough and cut 4 long strips 1/2" wide, placing them the length of the pan.
8. Cut 6 strips and place them crosswise to form a lattice top.
9. Bake 45 minutes in 350° oven.

NOTE: Serve cold with a small scoop of ice cream. This is a very rich dessert and small portions should be served.

Serves: 30
Preparation: 30 minutes
Cooking: 45 minutes

CHICKEN IN CLOVER

1 chicken
Broccoli
Cream sauce*
Grated cheese

1. Cook chicken and remove meat from bones.
2. Arrange toast at the bottom of a heat resistant dish or individual baking casserole.
3. Arrange cooked broccoli over toast, dark meat and then white meat.
4. Pour hot rich cream sauce over all.
5. Sprinkle with grated cheese.
6. Place under broiler until cheese is melted.

NOTE: String beans (whole), asparagus or brussel sprouts may be used in place of broccoli.

*Cream sauce—see glossary

Serves: 4-6
Preparation: 30 minutes
Cooking: 1 hour 30 minutes

VALCOUR LODGE
ON LAKE CHAMPLAIN

Tarley and Harold Lieberthal, owners of the historic Valcour Lodge, are prime examples of what this book is all about. One of the first to be interviewed, they serve as an inspiration throughout FAMOUS ADIRONDACK RESTAURANTS & RECIPES. Hearing Tarley's stories about the restaurant business made me realize much more what owning and managing a restaurant in our area really is all about.

The family of Tarley (Keith) Lieberthal were proprietors of the Royal Savage Inn. At only twelve years of age, she began waiting on tables at her family's restaurant. As she grew up, she met and married Harold. The Lieberthal family owned Valcour Lodge since 1938. She says, "I've never been without a restaurant."

Valcour is the famous historic site of the first major engagement of the Revolutionary War...The Battle of Valcour on October 11, 1776. Valcour Lodge bears testimony to the strong conviction the Lieberthal's have to preserve and share this ancestry. There are many antiques on display throughout the lounge and dining rooms.

Valcour Lodge is located just thirty-five miles south of Canada's border. The French influence is prevalent throughout northern New York and is featured as menu specialties. Harold and Tarley have various French appetizers and entrees, but, old favorites-steaks, chicken, veal and fresh seafood are also prepared from traditional American recipes which are cooked to perfection and tastefully served.

Harold is as much a part of the restaurant atmosphere as his food. He warmly greets each of his guests as they enter the cozy fireplace piano lounge and serves their requests with the confidence their dining experience will be pleasureable.

The Lieberthals are proud that Valcour Lodge is the first lakeside dining room on the New York State shore of Lake Champlain. Rustic cottages nestled in the cool pines and aromatic cedars are available for seasonal rentals.

Whether you choose an evening of dining or a summer vacation at the Valcour Lodge, you will enjoy meeting the personable Lieberthals. You cannot help feeling the Lieberthals' pride in their establishment which is so deeply steeped in the North Country heritage and tradition.

How to get there: *6 miles south of Plattsburgh. 6 miles north of AuSable Chasm. On Route 9 South. Panoramic cocktail deck overlooking the lake. Dinner. Cocktail Lounge. Cottages. (518) 563-3518.*

While you're there: *Swimming. Fishing. Boat moorings are available at the Lodge. Bluff Point championship golf course is located 1 mile north. A golf practice range operated by Day Brothers, also 1 mile north. Camping 3 miles south at a State Camp Park. Tennis at Clinton Community College 2 miles south. Above the Clinton Community College parking lot remarkable views of Vermont and the western edge of Lake Champlain can be seen.*

FILLET OF SOLE A LA AMIE

4 scallions
1/2 lb. fresh mushrooms
6 sprigs of parsley
4 T. butter
4 fillets of sole
3 T. lemon juice
3 T. white wine
3 T. bread crumbs

1. Sauté finely chopped scallions, mushrooms, parsley in butter.
2. Add Sole.
3. Sprinkle with lemon juice, wine and bread crumbs.
4. Sauté 5 or 6 minutes on each side.

Serves: 4
Preparation: 5 minutes
Cooking: 15 minutes

SAND CAKE

1 c. butter
1 c. confectionary sugar
1 c. fine sugar
4 eggs
3/4 c. cornstarch
3/4 c. cake flour
1 t. baking powder
1 t. vanilla
Rind of 1 lemon, finely grated

1. Preheat oven to 350 degrees. Flour and butter a 9" cake pan.
2. Cream butter and sugar together.
3. Add eggs one at a time, beating thoroughly.
4. Sift cornstarch, flour, baking powder together and mix thoroughly.
5. Add vanilla and lemon rind and mix batter well.
6. Pour into pan and bake 45 minutes or until toothpick comes out clean.
7. When cool, remove from pan and sprinkle with powdered sugar.

Serves: 12
Preparation: 15 minutes
Cooking: 45 minutes

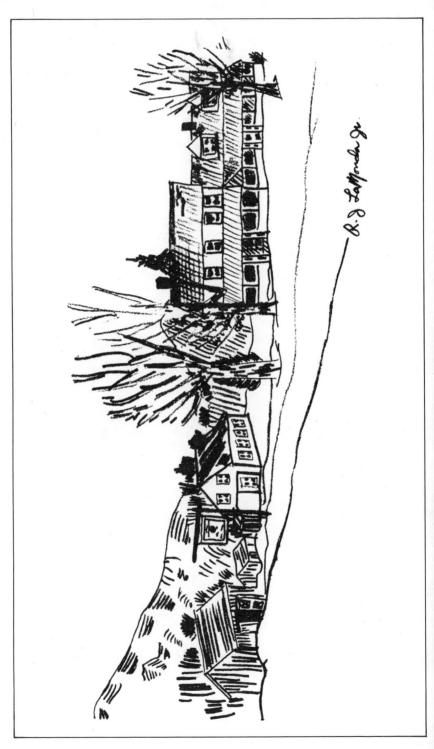

BARK EATER LODGE

The "Bark Eater Lodge" is certainly an older farmhouse that everyone would like to have as their own home. Deriving its name- "Bark Eater" from the Indian word meaning Adirondack, this small country inn was established in the early 1800's, when Keene was first being explored. The Inn has changed ownership only four times since its inception. It was located on the Old Military Road, the original road to Lake Placid, now renamed Alstead Mill Road, less than a mile off Route 73. Today it is hard to believe that the first "rail head" from Plattsburgh to Lake Placid was a three day trip by team.

Owned by the Wilson family since the 1930's, the operation of this charming inn was taken over in the 1970's by the team of Joe Pete Wilson and Harley McDevitt.

The Inn itself is a large old rambling farmhouse typical of New England style. It has a combination of hardwood and old wide boards floors. Furnishings of timeless beauty are in abundance.

The intimate atmosphere of the Bark Eater is quite unlike that of any restaurant. The old fashioned country gourmet food is served family style. Seated at one of the two large antique dining tables, Harley and Joe Pete join their guests for the meal. It is a dining event! You might enjoy the Spinach Salmon Roll, a specially baked pastry blended with spinach and salmon, dressed with a piquant dilled sour cream sauce. For dessert savor Pots-de-Creme, a light pastry shell filled with chocolate mousse, a touch of Kahlua topped with whipping cream and chocolate shavings.

Dining at the Bark Eater offers everyone not only a sumptuous meal and a first hand chance to meet other congenial people with similar interests, but the experience of sharing a meal with the lord and lady of the manor in their quaint cozy inn.

The quest to present its history as a rest stop for gourmet food, country charm, excellent service, gracious hosts, winter and summer activities, accessibility to the Adirondack Mountains and a change of pace has made the Bark Eater a winner of world wide fame. It is an Inn to be experienced and food to be savored time and time again.

How to get there: *From Keene on Route 73 driving toward Lake Placid, look for the sign on the right-Alstead Mill Road. About 1-2 miles from Keene. Reservations Only. Rooms. Cottages. Breakfast. Lunch. Dinner. (518) 576-2221.*

While you're there: *The Bark Eater has its own cross-country ski shop which offers rentals, lessons, tours and trail use. They participate in the Lodge-to-Lodge ski touring vacation. Horseback Riding. Hudson River Gorge whitewater rafting. Fishing. Hiking. If you're going to hike only one mountain in the Adirondacks, it should be Cascade Mountain located on Route 73, and one of the major 46 peaks of the Adirondacks. The well marked trail is located one mile east of Mt. Van Hoevenburg. It is a 2.5 mile hike and offers impressive views of about 30 other mountain peaks. While on Cascade Mountain, you can easily climb Porter Mountain as a side trip and have two major peaks in the same day.*

—— SPINACH SALMON ROLL ——

1/4 c. butter
1/2 c. flour
1-3/4 c. milk
1/2 t. salt
Dash of pepper
Dash of cayenne
5 egg yolks
5 egg whites
1/8 t. cream of tartar
1 package (9 oz.) frozen creamed spinach, thawed
1 can (16 oz.) salmon, drained and flaked
3/4 c. dill pickles, chopped
1 c. sour cream

1. Grease 15-1/2" x 10-1/2" jelly roll pan. Line bottom with wax paper. Grease and flour.
2. Melt butter in saucepan and mix in flour.
3. Gradually stir in milk, salt, pepper and cayenne.
4. Cook over medium heat, stirring constantly until sauce boils. Remove from heat.
5. Beat egg yolks. Stir in a small amount of sauce and return to saucepan. Cool to lukewarm.
6. Beat egg whites and cream of tartar until stiff but not dry. Fold into sauce.
7. Spread evenly in prepared pan. Bake in 400° oven for 30 minutes.
8. While roll is baking, combine spinach, salmon and pickles in medium sauce pan. Heat to simmering. Remove from heat.
9. After baking, loosen edge of roll with sharp knife, invert onto clean towel. Carefully pull off paper.
10. Spread filling on top. Roll jelly roll fashion from long sides.
11. Serve immediately with Dilled sour cream.

_ continued on next page _

DILLED SOUR CREAM

1. Combine 1 cup of sour cream and 2 tablespoons dill pickle liquid.

Serves: 8
Preparation: 3 minutes
Cooking: 3 minutes

NOTES

MORNING GLORY MUFFINS

2-1/2 c. sugar
4 c. flour
4 t. baking soda
4 t. cinnamon
1 t. salt
4 c. carrots, grated
1 c. raisins
1 c. pecans, chopped
1 c. sweetened coconut
2 apples grated and peeled
6 large eggs
2 c. vegetable oil
4 t. vanilla

1. Sift together sugar, flour, baking soda, cinnamon and salt.
2. Stir in carrots, raisins, pecans, coconut and apples.
3. In bowl beat eggs with vegetable oil and vanilla.
4. Stir into flour mixture until just combined.
5. Spoon batter into well buttered (1/3 cup) muffin tins, filling to the top.
6. Bake 350° for 35 minutes or until springy to touch.

Serves: 30
Preparation: 20 minutes
Cooking: 35 minutes

——— IRISH SODA BREAD ———

2 c. flour
1/4 c. sugar
1-1/2 t. baking powder
1/2 t. baking soda
Dash of salt
Raisins
1 c. buttermilk
1 stick oleo margarine

1. Combine flour, sugar, baking powder and soda, salt and raisins.
2. Add buttermilk and margarine by stirring.
3. Mold into loaf on baking sheet with edges.
4. Bake at 370° for 35-40 minutes.

Serves: 6
Preparation: 10 minutes
Cooking: 34-40 minutes

The Deer's Head Inn
Since 1808
The Adirondack's Oldest Inn

ELIZABETHTOWN

Millions of tourists visit Essex County each year. Celebrated as the most scenic county in northern New York State, Essex County offers travelers and residents unsurpassed vistas of mountains and lakes. Essex County encompasses the lofty high peaks of the Adirondack Mountains, the magnificent beauty of Lake Champlain renowned for its history of tragedy and heroism, and Lake Placid, a vacationer's paradise –– home of the 1932 and 1980 winter Olympics.

Housed in this beautiful county is the village of Elizabethtown, a destination for many who travel to this village to hunt in its mountains and woods, to fish in Lake Champlain, the brooks, the rivers, and the streams, to climb the oldest mountains in the United States, or just to relax away from the hustle and bustle of city life.

Vacations are always quality times and, for many, the modern conveniences coupled with charm and hospitality of a country inn are a "must." The Deer's Head Inn offers these "musts" and much more. Over 180 years old, the Inn is the oldest hotel in the Adirondacks, a good representative of the way things used to be, keeping the mood and decor of the original Inn from the early 1800's when it was built as a public house. It has been open ever since. It has been host to famous people such as Grover Cleveland, Benjamin Harrison, John L. Sullivan, and Daniel Webster. Mary Brown, wife of John Brown, arrived by sleigh in the dead of winter at Elizabethtown with the casket of her husband and the funeral party on December 7, 1859 on their last leg of the trek from Harpers Ferry to North Elba. Elisah Adams, then owner of the hotel, as well as Essex County sheriff, invited the Brown party to stay at the Inn. He suggested the body lie in state for the night in the courthouse directly across the street.

45

Though the Deer's Head Inn has changed for the sake of modernity, there are today, six sleeping rooms furnished with plenty of antiques and memorabilia which have accumulated over 180 years of active hostelry.

The Deer's Head Inn serves two meals a day, lunch and dinner, on the first floor of the Inn, Elizabethtown's best restaurant. All meals are open to the public. The lounge is more informal where sportsmen and business people often can be seen in lively conversation and fellowship.

Dining out is always special here, and the meals certainly enhance the experience of staying at the Inn. Some of the most asked-for entrees include Sauerbraten, a 16 ounce sirloin steak served with mushroom caps, wiener schnitzel, and mountain trout — all served on Blue Willow china reflecting the country atmosphere.

The Deer's Head Inn is one of those special places where you can set down your luggage, put up your feet and just relax. Here everything is low key and friendly. It is an Inn where you will enjoy a cooked-to-order adventure in dining, walk to a variety of shops, and still be minutes away from more mountain peaks than you could ever climb.

How to get there: *Off I-87, take Exit 31 and follow sign 4 miles to Elizabethtown. The Inn is on Main Street. Rooms. Lunch. Dinner. Lounge. (518) 873-9995.*

While you're there: *Cobble Hill Golf Course offers a pleasant 9 hole course. Adirondack Museum is located in the center of Elizabethtown, a worthy trip. Carpenter's Painters and Art Gallery is located 2 or 3 miles north of Elizabethtown. The Meadowmount School of Music offers free concerts on Wednesday and Sunday evenings during the summer months. Hiking. Hunting. Fishing. Camping. A good place to gather blueberries in the late summer is on the east trail to Giant Mountain which starts 1.3 miles south of Elizabethtown on Highway 9, south of the New Russia post office. When you reach "The Cobbles," a 1.8 miles clearly marked trail, you will see hundreds of blueberry bushes among the rocks. You'll need a bucket!*

CHILI CON CARNE

2 lbs. ground beef
2 medium onions, minced
2 green peppers, minced
4 stalks celery, chopped fine
2 qt. tomato sauce
2 – 12 oz. cans kernel corn
Garlic salt to taste
Cayenne pepper to taste
Salt and fresh black ground pepper to taste

1. In large skillet sauté first 4 items until ground beef is well done.
2. Drain off excess fat.
3. Add remaining ingredients and season to taste with garlic salt, salt, cayenne pepper and fresh ground pepper.
4. Serve over rice with hot garlic bread on the side.
CHEF'S NOTE: This can be served over pasta or potatoes in place of rice.

Serves: 8
Preparation: 5 minutes
Cooking: 20 minutes

ALAN'S CREAM CHICKEN BREAST

1 medium onion, minced fine
2 — 12 oz. cans cream of chicken soup
2 — 12 oz. cans cream of mushroom soup
1 — 16 oz. pot of sour cream
1/2 pt. milk
8—10 pieces of chicken breast

1. In large bowl mix together first 5 items.
2. Place chicken in a large roasting pan and cover with mixture.
3. Bake at 350 degree oven until chicken is cooked about 30 minutes or more.
4. Serve over rice, pasta, or boiled potatoes.

Serves: 8—10
Preparation: 5 minutes
Cooking: 30—45 minutes

BAKED PEACH CRUMBLE

1 c. sliced peaches, fresh or canned
1/2 c. melted butter
10 graham cracker squares, crushed
1/2 c. rolled oats
1/4 c. sugar
1/2 t. cinnamon

1. Place peaches and juice in a 8" pan.
2. Mix together the remaining ingredients.
3. Cover the peaches and juice.
4. Bake in 375 degree oven for 25 minutes.
5. Serve with whipped cream or ice cream.

Serves: 6
Preparation: 10 minutes
Cooking: 25 minutes

ELM TREE INN

KEENE

The Elm Tree Inn is more than a restaurant nestled in the Adirondacks-it is the Adirondacks! The charm of this older Essex County Inn is derived, not only, from its rusticity or reputation for good, American style food, but also, because of a long standing North Country legend about a famous Elm Tree.

During a visit to the 1932 Lake Placid Olympic games, young Monty Purdy developed a great love for the Adirondacks and its people. In 1946, Purdy, with his wife and three children, left his Rochester home to settle in the Keene valley. The family then purchased the existing inn and began the task of rebuilding its reputation as one of providing travel weary people with good, home-cooked meals and the opportunity to meet and socialize in a pleasant and relaxed setting.

In front of the Inn stood a majestic Elm tree-one "legends are made of." The tree, one of the largest Elms in Eastern United States, had a girth of twenty one and one-half feet and measured just under one hundred feet high. In the late fifties, the tree became the victim of the dreaded Dutch Elm disease. With plenty of TLC from all the Purdy's, the tree survived until October 1974. The day the tree was cut down, Monty asked the men cutting the tree to leave a stump twelve feet high so he could have the largest stump in the Adirondack Park. At the base of the tree lies the following poem:

51

The Elm

"Caesar saw fifty years
For centuries I have stood and
watched
The ceaseless flow of generations
Beneath my branches to and fro
As savage, pioneer and tourist
know."

Today, Monty's son Ron and his sister Bev, continue his tradition for excellence in running the Elm Tree Inn.

The Inn is renown for its soups: corn chowder, tuna chowder, mushroom, pea or vegetable. The kitchen is also famous for its Purdyburger, an oversized hamburger topped with a slice of onion and completely covered with melted cheese. They have a special way of making the common hamburger the most uncommon, delicious sandwich that you have tasted.

The rustic decor features a glowing fireplace in the outer room. Fast moving conversation at the bar and photos covering the walls of the two dining rooms depict the Purdy's lifelong interest in bobsledding and the Elm Tree Inn.

The restaurant proves that frills and fancy decor are not necessary to a winning establishment. Purdy's Elm Tree Inn is more than a legend, or an institution...it IS the Adirondacks.

How to get there: Elm Tree Inn is located at the intersection of Rtes. 73 and 9N in Keene, N.Y. Lunch. Dinner. Lounge.

While you're there: Hiking the forty six major peaks in New York State is nearby. Day Hikes. The summit of Nubble is a 1.4 mile marked trail. The hike begins at Chapel Pond on Highway 73, 3 miles south of Keene Valley. (Keene and Keene Valley are two separate villages) You can also begin a longer hike (1.8 mile approach) beginning at Roaring Brook Falls parking lot, one mile west of Chapel Pond. It offers breathtaking views of "the Great Range." Fishing. Canoeing. An annual canoe race starts in Keene and goes to Jay. It is usually held in May.

MUSHROOM SOUP

1 lb. fresh mushrooms
1 can evaporated milk
Salt and pepper

1. Slice fresh mushrooms.
2. Cover and boil 10 minutes.
3. Thicken to the consistency of pancake batter with flour.
4. Thin with evaporated milk to desired thickness.
5. Add salt and pepper to taste.

Serves: 4
Preparation: 15 minutes

MOUNTAIN STEAK

1-1/2 c. Ritz crackers
4 cube steaks
6 eggs
3/4 c. evaporated milk
Butter
Salt and pepper

1. Grind fine the Ritz crackers
2. Mix together eggs, milk, salt and pepper.
3. Dip cube steaks in mixture.
4. Coat with the crackers.
5. Fry in a skillet on medium heat with a large amount of butter.

Serves: 4
Preparation: 20 minutes

THE WESTPORT YACHT CLUB

WESTPORT

The Village of Westport is a small friendly town tucked unassumingly on the shores of beautiful Lake Champlain. To the West are the Adirondack Mountains and to the East across the lake are the Green Mountains of Vermont.

As early as 1880 the well-to-do Summer visitor began to arrive to this small village and the Westport Yacht Club was very much a part of the reason why. Back then, the Yacht Club held parties, Saturday night dances and regattas on the lake. Residents and visitors remember those times as happy occasions of light style fun.

In February 1982 the Yacht Club was completely destroyed by fire. The owners, the Bradamant Corporation, immediately rebuilt a new replica of the original club and reopened in the Summer of '83. Today, the Yacht Club is as lively, during the Summer months as ever.

The best thing about the Club is the open air deck where you can enjoy the spectacular mountain views and watch the seagulls and sailboats while relaxing with a favorite drink, appetizers or a delicious meal.

Inside the restaurant carries through the nautical theme with an air of sophistication. In addition to the lovely sea style dining room, on the second floor there is a spacious banquet room and a fully equipped conference room for special events and meetings.

As you might expect, the food is as genuine as the atmosphere and service. Everything is made from scratch. Entree choices include succulent steaks or fresh seafood, such as sweet and sour shrimp served on a bed of rice. The steaks are cooked perfectly, as well as, the other taste tempting choices on the menu.

Whether you have come to stay in Westport's unhurried atmosphere for the summer or a few days, or you are traveling north or south, The Westport Yacht Club gives a new meaning to going to the beach. The restaurant provides a panoramic view, delicious food and relaxation at the water's edge...a perfect ending to a day at the beach.

How to get there: *The Westport Yacht Club is located on Old Arsenal Road. From Interstate 87, Exit 31, drive east on 9N to the village. Just south past the Inn on the Library Lawn on the left hand side is Old Arsenal Road. Follow down to the end of the road. Dinner. Cocktails (518) 962-8777.*

While you're here: *You can walk off some of your meal on the beach or Westport's historical walking tour of the village. Swimming. Golf. Tennis. Boating. 4th of July parade including a boat parade. Community picnics open to the public. Cross country skiing. Winter Carnival.*

DILL DIP

1 pint of mayonnaise
1 pint of sour cream
3 T. minced fresh parsley
3 T. minced onions
3 T. dill weed
1-1/2 t. seasoning salt

1. Mix together and refrigerates.
2. Make a couple of days in advanced.
3. Serve with Fresh veggies.

Makes: 2 pints

STEAK MARINADE

1 c. soy sauce
2 large onions coarsely chopped
2 cloves of garlic, halved
1/4 c. kitchen bouquet
1 tsp. accent
1/2 t. Lawry's seasoned salt

1. Mix ingredients together.
2. Marinade steak for at least 1/2 hour.

Preparation: 5 minutes

BEER BATTER ONION RINGS

1 onion sliced in rings
1 flat 12 oz. bottle of beer *al dk German* *lots of yeast*
Flour
1 tsp. granulated garlic
1 t. onion salt
1 t. salt
1 t. pepper
1/2 c. cornstarch

1. Mix all ingredients thoroughly except cornstarch.
2. Dip onion slices in cornstarch, then in batter.
3. Deep fry at 350.

NOTE: Rings will float on top and must be turned once.

Serves: 1
Preparation: 10 minutes
Cooking: 3 minutes

SWEET AND SOUR SHRIMP

12 shrimp
1/4 green pepper, julienne
1 pineapple ring, diced
6 water chestnuts, canned
1 T. butter
12 oz. pineapple juice
3 oz. wine vinegar
1-1/2 c. sugar

1. Boil pineapple juice, vinegar and sugar until it starts to thicken.
2. Take 4 oz. of sauce and 1 T. butter and saute over medium heat.
3. Add shrimp, peeled and deveined, with green pepper, pineapple and chestnuts.
4. Cook until shrimp are done (shrimp will turn a solid white). You may want to lower heat and use a cover.

Serves: 1
Preparation: 20 minutes

WHITEFACE CHALET

WILMINGTON

At the base of majestic Whiteface Mountain nestled in a hundred acres of white birches and pine woods, you will discover The Whiteface Chalet. The architecture and location reminds one of a scene in the Swiss Alps. The dining room has an adjoining living room with television and an assortment of toys. Realizing that a short wait for dinner is sometimes difficult for youngsters, they are invited to use the facilities until the meal is served. This unique arrangement makes dining more pleasant for the entire family. Often you will find the parents enjoying the magnificent view and some adult conversation over a cup of coffee while the children are playing in the next room. This informal atmosphere is relaxing and so refreshing!

Meals are meticulously prepared. Breakfast is always a treat at the Chalet. Buttermilk pancakes or cinnamon french toast is the perfect way to start your day. Baskets of breads are served at the table with your own toaster nearby to ensure that your toast is hot and done just the way that you like it. The salad bar is set up nightly with over twenty items including homemade house dressings and all the ingredients for a king size tossed salad. The soup du jour and special desserts, such as; the cream puffs, rum cake and the "secret recipe" cheesecake, have been lauded by gourmets from all over the world. The menu has a pleasing variety of steaks, chops, fish, and chicken with a daily chef's special.

An extra bonus is the ground level rustic bar and lounge where you will often find a group singing along around the piano or chatting by the fireplace. The pool and ping-pong games have been the scene of some fierce competition. A feeling of comraderie and friendliness abide in this

61

family oriented chalet.

A few days stay in this delightful mountain chalet will leave you peacefully relaxed and always looking forward to your next visit.

How to get there: *The Whiteface Chalet is on Springfield Road in Wilmington, N.Y. about one mile east of Route 86. Breakfast. Lunch. Dinner. Lounge. Rooms. Tennis courts. Swimming pool. (518) 946-2207.*

While you're there: *Fishing. Hiking. Attractions. It is within minutes to Santa's Workshop, High Falls Gorge and the Whiteface Memorial Highway. During July and August there is a Science Lecture Series held at the Science Lodge on the Memorial Highway in Wilmington. It is held every Tuesday at 8:30 P.M.. Copperas Pond Trail begins on Highway 86, three miles south of the Whiteface Ski Area's parking lot. Look for the trail marker on the east side. The short half-mile walk makes it a perfect isolated wilderness lake for picnics, family walks, complete with two original lean-tos. The pond has high rocks for diving and sunbathing.*

BAKED RED SNAPPER FILET

2-8 oz. Snapper filets
1 tomato, thinly sliced
1 onion, thinly sliced
1/4 c. butter, melted
1/2 t. parsley
1/8 t. oregano

1. Place each filet in center of a large piece of aluminum.
2. Arrange slices of tomato and onion alternately overlapping slightly.
3. Pour several tablespoons of melted butter over fish and sprinkle with parsley and oregano.
4. Bake wrapped loosely in foil, tightly closed for 45 minutes at 325° until fish is flaky.
5. Serve with lemon wedges.

Serves: 2
Preparation: 5 minutes
Cooking: 45 minutes

BEEF STROGANOFF A LA CHALET

6 T. flour
3 t. salt
1/2 t. pepper
2 lbs. beef tenderloin
2 garlic cloves
1/4 c. butter
1 c. onions, minced
1/2 c. water
2 cans condensed chicken soup, undiluted
2 lbs. fresh mushrooms, sliced
2 c. sour cream
Snipped parsley

1. Trim all fat from meat.
2. Rub with garlic cloves.
3. Combine flour, salt and pepper and pound into meat.
4. Cut beef into 1-1/2" x 1" strips.
5. Brown meat in butter in a Dutch oven. (Watch carefully to prevent burning. Turn often.)
6. Add onions and sauté until golden brown.
7. Add water, soup and mushrooms.
8. Cook over low heat, stirring occasionally until tender.
9. Add sour cream just before serving over hot noodles.

Serves: 8
Preparation: 30 minutes

RUM NUT CAKE

2 c. sugar
1 c. butter, softened
3-1/2 c. cake flour
1 c. milk
6 egg yolks
1-1/2 t. double acting baking powder
2 t. vanilla
1/8 t. salt
1 c. pecans, chopped
1/2 c. dark rum

GLAZE

1/3 c. butter
1/4 c. water
1 c. sugar
1/2 c. dark rum

1. Sprinkle nuts on bottom of pan.
2. In a large bowl, mix sugar and butter with mixer at high speed until light and fluffy.
3. Add the rest of the ingredients.
4. Mix at low speed until well mixed.
5. Beat at high speed for 4 minutes.
6. Bake in 350° oven for 1 hour or until toothpick comes out clean.
7. Cool on rack.
   GLAZE
8. Melt butter and add sugar and water.
9. Boil 5 minutes stirring constantly.
10. Remove from heat and add rum.
11. Place cooled cake on rack in a large pan.
12. Prick deeply with fork or skewer.
13. Baste with glaze and keep pouring glaze from pan into container and use to continue basting until all the glaze is used up.

_continued on next page _

14. Serve with a dollop of whipped cream on each slice. Garnish with chopped nuts and a cherry.

NOTE: This is very good served with a hard sauce.

Serves: 12
Preparation: 30 minutes
Cooking: 1 hour/15 minutes

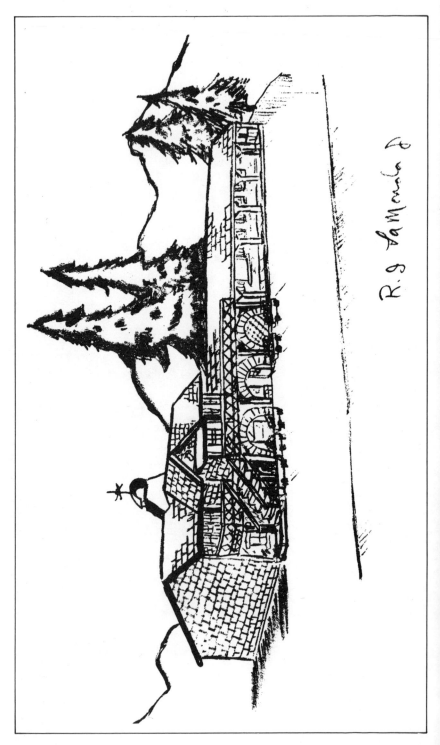

ALPINE CELLAR
RESTAURANT

LAKE PLACID

Old European Charm are the words most appropriate in describing The Alpine Cellar. Located in Lake Placid on Route 86 one-fourth mile past the traffic light (it is the only traffic light in town and is at the junction of Routes 86 and 73,) The Alpine Cellar has been an overwhelming success with area residents and visitors alike.

Monique and Wolfgang Brandenburg are the two people who have made it so successful and it hasn't taken them long either. They are a very talented twosome. Meeting at a party in New York City, they soon married and settled in Lake Placid. Monique is an interior designer and her talent is very noticeable throughout the restaurant. Wolfgang is a chef, having studied at the chef's school in Frankfort, Germany. With the two combining their talents, they have diligently worked to maintain the high standards their restaurant is noted for. Wolfgang is one of the few area chefs of the International organization.

Dining at The Alpine Cellar is a "holiday in Europe" at only a fraction of the cost. A comfortable atmosphere surrounds you as if you were vacationing in Switzerland or Germany. From the handpainted murals on the ceiling, to the handcarved beams, to wooden carvings, to the evident antique oversized cowbell, The Alpine Cellar is filled with authentic charm. The menu includes excellent steaks and seafood as well as superbly prepared German favorites of Sauerbraten, Rouladen, Wienerschnitzel and Kassler Rippchen. Nothing is overlooked by the watchful eyes of Monique and Wolfgang in their pursuit to provide you with a unique dining experience. From the Bavarian beer barrel bar, to the cocktail waitress' traditional dirndled dress, to the comfortable captain's chairs, The Alpine Cellar is truly a dining adventure.

Monique's decorating talents are again evident in the very private Swiss dining room with tables and booths of light wood color overlooking a picturesque view of the Adirondack Mountains.

Monique and Wolfgang take great pride in making your visit a happy and memorable one. And for me, The Alpine Cellar will always be remembered as one of my favorite travel adventures.

How to get there: *Go to the traffic light at the junction of Route 86, just 200 yards. Rooms. Lounge opens at 3 PM. Dinner. (518) 523-2180.*

While you're there: *Lake Placid is a year round resort with attractions in all seasons. For a days outing, you can visit the Olympic ski jump. Take a ride to the top. Lunch at the bobsled and luge run. Also Hiking. Fishing. Boat rides. Mountain Views. For those families with small children or those who want a short hike, less than a mile, Mt. Jo is the perfect choice. It is a mountain that offers priceless views. The trail begins at the Adirondack Lodge at Heart Lake, off Route 73. The view from the summit is one of the best in the Adirondacks for the least amount of climbing.*

SAUERBRATEN

2-1/2 pounds rump or chuck roast
3 c. water
1 c. vinegar
1 T. sugar
1 small onion, minced
1 stalk celery, finely chopped
pinch of salt
pinch mixed spices
6-8 crushed gingersnaps

1. Marinade meat for 4 days, turning daily.
2. Brown meat and add marinade.
3. Roast until meat is tender, about 2 hours.
4. Remove meat. Add gingersnaps to marinade and make gravy to desired consistency. Serve with sliced meat.

Serves: 4-6
Preparation: 4 days
Cooking: 2 hours

WIENER SCHNITZEL

3-1/2-4 pounds veal steak
3/4 t. salt
1/8 t. pepper
2 eggs
1/2 c. milk
3/4 t. salt
2 T. flour
1 c. dry bread crumbs, finely sifted

1. Flatten veal with wooden meat tenderizer.
2. Combine salt and pepper and sprinkle meat.
3. Blend beaten eggs, milk, salt and flour.
4. Dip meat in this mixture and then in bread crumbs.
5. Fry in hot shortening 6-7 minutes on each side.

Lard ? Peanut Oil? (Avacado Oil?)

Serves: 4
Preparation: 10 minutes
Cooking: 12 minutes

*Serve with S+ Sour Beets
+ Home made German Noodles
mch in Pantry*

RED CABBAGE

4 bacon strips
1 small head red cabbage, finely cut
1 medium apple, finely chopped
1 small onion, fincly chopped
1 T. salt
1/4 c. sugar
3/4 c. vinegar
2 c. water
A few cloves
1 bay leaf

1. Sauté bacon in kettle.
2. Add remaining ingredients and cook until tender.

Serves: 6
Preparation: 10 minutes
Cooking: About 15 minutes

ARTIST'S CAFE

LAKE PLACID

Lake Placid is a beautiful lake resort community surrounded by the Adirondack Mountains. It is nestled within the high peaks of Mount Marcy, Whiteface Mountain, rolling foothills, evergreens and miles of clean lakes, rivers and streams. The mountains are majestic and the terrain is woodsy. Camping areas are plentiful. They are rustic and offer you comfort and privacy. Unlike most camping grounds in the United States, you won't be the only one with a tent.

While in Lake Placid, browsing and shopping can carry away an entire day. Fashions are sporty, classic and very stylish. Antiques, books, clothing, collectibles and souvenirs fill the shops in beautiful displays.

While there, the Artist's Cafe is a "must stop." Ed and Joan Kane and their three sons, Fred, Rob and Willie acquired the restaurant two years ago changing the menu only to improve it by adding their own special creations.

You will find the Artist's Cafe located at the very beginning of Main Street on the lakeside. You'll walk down a full flight of stairs and receive a warm, friendly greeting from one of the Kanes who will seat you in the cozy dining room or on the porch where you can enjoy the captivating scenes of Mirror Lake.

The Cafe's menu varies slightly between lunch and dinner. Many enjoy the "create your own" omelette made with ham, bacon, cheese, chives and mushrooms. For the beef lovers, there is the Cafe Cheese Steak, thinly sliced beef with onions covered with melted cheese served on a special Italian roll. The dinner menu includes some of the same offerings priced no higher than lunch, with a few additions, including:

74

New York cut Sirloin Steak, Scampi a la Biff and Chicken turnovers. Their own steak fries, which are included with most meals, are perfectly fried tender on the inside, brown and crunchy on the outside-seasoned just right. Nowhere in the Adirondacks will you find this special way of preparation that makes them so good.

For a sweet ending, there is a diversity of splendid, rich desserts, and as many dessert coffees. Whatever you order at the Artist's Cafe, you will receive delicious hungry size portions expertly prepared.

Pictured on the walls of this small forty eight seat restaurant are many black and white print scenes of the Adirondack area and are for sale.

Visit this favorite corner cafe in Lake Placid. From the moment you arrive pleasing aromas from the kitchen fill the room. Surely it is a splendid way to enjoy a perfect lunch or dinner.

How to get there: *1 Main St., Lake Placid. Lunch. Dinner. Cocktail Bar. (518) 523-9493.*

While you're there: *Mountain camping. Boating. All Winter and Summer sports. Attractions. Hiking. Theatre. A swim in Mirror Lake will have you ready for canoeing or sailing or any of the other water sports. Boat Tours.*

SCAMPI A LA BIFF

7 large shrimp, peeled and deveined
2 t. lemon juice
3 T. butter
1/4 c. white wine
1/2 c. mushrooms
1 T. cognac
1 clove of garlic, crushed
1 fresh shallot

1. Saute shrimp in lemon juice.
2. Add butter, shallot, garlic and wine.
3. Add cognac and mushrooms.
4. Continue to saute until shrimp is cooked through and mushrooms are done.
5. Serve over rice.

NOTE: William Tennant introduced this to the Kanes.

Serves: 1
Preparation: 20 minutes

Wine (white?)

CAFE POTATO SKINS

2 baked potatoes, sliced lengthwise and hollowed out. Save potato.
1/4 c. onions, chopped
1/4 c. green pepper
1/4 c. cooked bacon
2 T. cheddar cheese
Leftover potato
Butter

1. Sauté all ingredients in butter until onion is translucent.
2. Fill hollowed out skins with mixture.
3. Cover with cheddar cheese.
4. Put under broiler until cheese is bubbly and starts to brown on top.

Serves: 1
Preparation: 10 minutes
Cooking: 2-3 minutes

NOTES

THE "GOBBLER" SANDWICH

1 Hoagie roll
5 oz. turkey breast
1/4 c. raw mushrooms
2 slices tomato
Lettuce
Alfalfa sprouts
2 strips cooked bacon
1/4 c. cheddar cheese
1 T. butter

1. Toast roll.
2. Layer lettuce, turkey, tomato, mushrooms, bacon, sprouts.
3. Top with cheddar cheese.
4. Put under broiler until cheese melts.

Serves: 1
Preparation: 10 minutes

NOTES

the Woodshed

LAKE PLACID

Ah...Lake Placid. It is a sanctuary of natural beauty created by crystal-clear Lake Placid and Mirror Lake along with acres of undeveloped forests and some of the oldest mountains in North America. Lake Placid is almost undiscovered by the many vacationers who are looking for a quiet respite for a week or two.

As you enter Lake Placid's Main Street from the East, you'll discover the charming Woodshed restaurant. Opened by Terry Ziff in 1985, the Woodshed receives mountains of applause from Lake Placid residents and visitors alike. It is a type of restaurant where you can enjoy a light lunch or sandwich served in the front dining room named Lindsay's. At Lindsay's one experiences a rustic dining room which is decorated with Tiffany lamps, antiques, and white linen covered tables. The exquisite food is prepared by chef-owner Terry Ziff, a graduate of the Culinary Institute of America, and chef Joe Martin, one of the best chefs in Lake Placid. Both men are the keys to the success of the restaurant. They are trained in classic and French cuisines which definitely shows up on the menu. Both men like to emphasize seasonal foods using the freshest ingredients obtainable. All the dishes are homemade right there in the kitchen including desserts and breads. It is good to know that Terry and Joe simply will not compromise the high standards that they have set for themselves as they work in their kitchen.

Some of the appetizers offered are Quail Fermiere, Pate Maison, Shrimp Dijon, and Escargot Maison en Bouchee. They all are marvelous! One salad delight is the delicious creamy dill; another is the lemon Ceasar complete with snappy greens. Both the creamy Shrimp Bisque and the fresh salad look like they belong on the cover of a food magazine. The entrees, too, are fine works of art whether it is poached salmon in white wine, a delicious veal dish, the supreme of chicken with sauce Choron with wild rice stuffing, or steak au poivre verte which is prime filet mignon, cognac, green peppercorns and cream. The vegetables give a nice balance.

Desserts are not to be missed. One of the most irresistible delights in the Adirondacks is Terry's famous white chocolate mousse. It is an ultra elegant piece de resistance brought to your table by one of the friendly waiters who serves you with plenty of finesse.

Lindsay's at the Woodshed is truly a culinary experience not to be missed, but do get reservations so you won't be disappointed as the dining room seats only 52 people. Come hungry! At the Woodshed there are so many wonderful foods that enable guests to experience the art of Lake Placid dining at its very best!

How to get there: *237 Main St. on the east end of the Village. Front dining room for light lunches. Lindsay's, the back dining room, has a full menu. Open 7 days a week. 518-523-9470.*

While you're there: *Boat cruises. Mountain climbing. Golfing. Swimming. Boating. Fishing. Horseback riding. Theater. Nearby is Mount Whitney, where skiing first started in America. It is opened for day and night skiing. Whiteface Mountain, just a few miles from Lake Placid, offers some of the best skiing in the East. Bobsledding. Ice skating.*

ESCARGOT MAISON EN BOUCHEE

12 escargot (French burgundy snails)
1-1/2 c. heavy cream
1 t. garlic, minced
1 t. shallots, chopped fine
1 t. parsley, freshly chopped
Salt
Pepper
1/2 oz. white wine (Chablis)
1/4 oz. brandy

1. Combine all ingredients in sauce pot and bring to a medium boil.
2. Cook uncovered for approximately 5-7 minutes at a constant boil.
3. The sauce will reduce down by two thirds and will be slightly thickened.
4. To serve, heat pastry shell on serving dish and place 6 escargot on each shell. Pour sauce over top.

NOTE: The sauce should be bubbling hot on the serving dish when it is served.

Serves: 2
Preparation: 15 minutes
Cooking time: 5-7 minutes

FRESH DILL DRESSING

1 quart mayonnaise
1-1/2 c. sour cream
2 T. fresh dill, chopped
3 T. grated Parmesan cheese
1-1/2 t. crushed black pepper
3/4 t. garlic, minced
1 T. worcestershire sauce
3 T. onion, grated
1-1/2 t. salt

1. Combine all ingredients and mix well.
2. Finish with milk to achieve desired consistency.

NOTE: Fresh dill makes the difference.

Yields: 1 quart
Preparation: 10-15 minutes

LOBSTER CANCUN WITH SAUCE BISCAYNE

4 Australian lobster tails (or any cold water lobster tails)
4 boneless chicken breasts, skinless
Flour
Bread crumbs, fine, seasoned
Eggwash (egg and milk)

1. Remove lobster from the tails.
2. Bone and skin chicken breasts.
3. Lightly pound each chicken breast to tenderize and to increase the size for easy wrapping of each lobster tail.
4. Wrap each chicken breast around each lobster tail.
5. Bread each one by dusting with flour, dip in eggwash and then bread crumbs.
6. Place on baking pan and sprinkle with melted butter.
7. Bake at 350° for 20 minutes.
8. Slice into medallions and arrange on serving plate.
9. Coat lightly with Sauce Biscayne.

continued on next page

SAUCE BISCAYNE

1 lb. raw shrimp, medium or large
1/2 lemon
1 bay leaf
1 t. paprika
1 small onion, diced
1/4 c. Madeira wine or sherry
Roux - 2 oz. flour and 2 oz. butter

1. Place shrimp in sauce pot with cold water (4-5 cups) to cover by 2 inches.
2. Squeeze lemon and place it in the shrimp. Yes, the entire lemon to get full zest.
3. Season with salt and pepper and add bay leaf.
4. Place on stove and bring to a boil.
5. Remove immediately and reserve liquid for sauce (Shrimp may be used for shrimp cocktail, shrimp salad, etc.).
6. Dice onion and saute in butter.
7. Add paprika and roux and stir constantly.
8. Add hot shrimp liquid and whip until sauce is a smooth consistency.
9. Season with salt, pepper and wine.
10. Simmer 15 minutes. Strain sauce.
11. Coat lobster cancun.

Serves: 4
Preparation: 1 hour
Cooking: 30 minutes

THE CHARCOAL PIT

LAKE PLACID

Just as the exploration of the Adirondacks led thousands to climbing the high peaks in the 1900's, the same anticipation brings thousands of tourists to Lake Placid to explore its wide variety of sporting events, clear lakes, antique, art and gift shops, museums, attractions and gourmet restaurants.

The many Lake Placid restaurants feature a vast variety of cuisine combining ancestorial backgrounds with the art of cooking, bringing up some of the best dining in Northern New York. The Charcoal Pit is always included among the many restaurants recommended by residents and friends who visit Lake Placid often.

The Charcoal Pit, owned by the Hadjis' family opened their gourmet restaurant in 1954. It is operated by Jimmy Hadjis who is the chef, manager and part owner. His sister is the Maitre'd and his Mother still is involved in some of the baking.

The Charcoal Pit is located just outside the village of Lake Placid on the Sara-Placid Road. The spacious restaurant is decorated with many green plants, dark stained beams and centered in the main dining room is a false skylight. For privacy, an intimate "VIP" glass enclosed room accommodates ten to twelve people. If you prefer your cocktail served separate from dining, a small lounge offers a cordial atmosphere.

Jimmy, having graduated in the tenth class of Paul Smith's Culinary and Restaurant program, has been cooking for thirty years. He is always experimenting with new original recipes which lends to the interesting variety on the menu.

His menu includes as many seafood entrees as beef with usually two or three special evening offerings. One such entree is the Shrimp Francine. It is an authentic recipe invented by Jimmy and is named after his wife. Nothing is prepared ahead of time except the soups and desserts. The cheesecake and Mousse are homebaked by Jimmy's mother.

Dining at The Charcoal Pit is a festive celebration, for whatever is good in life. Jimmy and his family want to share their zest for life in quality meals, good companionship, and relaxation, set in beautiful surroundings, offering more than just another meal. At The Charcoal Pit, it is an evening of luxurious pleasure.

How to get there: Route 86 on the Sara-Placid highway. Dinner. Cocktail Lounge. Children's menu. (518) 523-3050.

While you're there: On Saranac Avenue is the Center for Music, Drama and Art which houses a modern stage theater, an art gallery, a library of the arts, an art supply store, a lecture hall and classrooms. Year round they offer professional and community activities. Lake Placid offers many sporting events, festivals, parades. Hiking. Boating. Touring. Attractions.

ESCARGOT PROVENCALE

1 can French snails (24 to a can)
1/4 lb. of butter
1 T. shallots
1/4 t. salt
1/4 t. white pepper
4 oz. sweet sherry wine
1 t. chives
24 snail shells

1. Drain juice from can.
2. Melt butter and saute shallots until they are translucent.
3. Salt and pepper.
4. Add snails and chives. Stir.
5. Slowly add sweet sherry to pan and allow liquid to reduce to one half or until liquid thickens.
6. Place each snail in a shell deep enough to allow room for garlic butter.

GARLIC BUTTER

8 oz. butter soft, but not melted.
4-5 cloves of garlic (minced)
2 T. parsley (chopped fine)

1. Mix all ingredients together to form the garlic butter.
2. Fill each shell.
3. Place on escargot dish and bake in 350° oven, until butter begins to bubble, about 15 minutes.

NOTE: You may also prepare escargot ahead of time and freeze for later use.

Serves: 4
Preparation: 20 minutes
Cooking: 10/15 minutes

SHRIMP SCAMPI

24 shrimp, large
8 fresh garlic cloves, minced
1/2 lb. butter, melted
2 c. sweet sherry wine
Salt and pepper
Paprika

1. Peel and butterfly shrimp down the back and clean with fresh water.
2. Place shrimp on a heavy metal hot plate, tails up. Or you may saute shrimp on low to medium heat on stove top.
3. Place butter in saute pan and melt on low heat.
4. Add minced garlic, shrimp and saute together on medium heat along with a sprinkling of salt and pepper.
5. When shrimp have turned white and appear to be cooked, add sherry wine slowly so as not to catch fire from the alcohol content.
6. Allow to reduce liquid to one-half.
7. Add paprika for color. Stir.

NOTE: Serve with steamed rice.

Serves: 4
Preparation: 15 minutes
Cooking: 15 minutes

SEAFOOD STUFFING

3 c. cold water
16 oz. salad shrimp, bits and pieces
1 t. thyme
3 oz. red onion, minced
5 oz. butter
5 oz. flour
1/8 oz. fresh parsley, minced
1 t. garlic, granulated
1 t. salt
1 c. sweet sherry wine or Marsala wine
Pinch of pepper
8 oz. Snowcrab meat
8 oz. Sea sticks

1. Bring to boil cold water, salad shrimp and thyme. Set aside.
2. Melt butter over low heat, add onion and saute until onion is transparent, about 5 minutes. Add parsley and slowly add flour, constantly stirring with a wire whip or large spoon so not to burn.
3. Add 2-1/2 cups of shrimp stock previously boiled and set aside. Add garlic, salt and pepper, constantly stirring. As mixture begins to thicken, add wine, continually stirring. This may be done on medium heat. You must constantly stir this or it will burn. SHUT OFF HEAT.
4. Add Snowcrab meat and Sea sticks (chopped medium course). Thoroughly mix. Drain the rest of the stock off the shrimp and add just the shrimp to the mixture. Place in a shallow pan, cover with plastic wrap and refrigerate.

NOTE: Very good for stuffing fresh fish such as fillet of sole or trout, shrimp, chicken breasts, veal medallions. You may top your fish or shrimp dish with Newburg sauce. Chicken and veal may be topped with a nice Mornay sauce and served.

Serves: 8
Preparation: 25 minutes

FREDERICK'S

LAKE PLACID

The Adirondack Park is the ideal choice for a vacation considering the climate, elevation and natural attractions. There are over 2000 lakes and over 2000 mountains and one of the world's greatest forests. Lake Placid Village with a population of only 5000 residents is a thriving year round community. Known as a major sports capital throughout the United States, Lake Placid has hosted the Winter Olympics in 1932 and again in 1980. It is now one of two Olympic Training Centers in the entire country and why not! All the facilities are there and maintained at the high standard that the athletes require.

Olympian athletes also need high standards in what they eat and Frederick's Restaurant on Signal Hill offers just those standards of excellence.

A family operated gourmet restaurant is originally part of the historic Stevens House Hotel complex which was torn down in 1945, only to have Nancy and Fred Richards develop this quiet retreat overlooking Lake Placid and the MacKenzie Mountain Range. Exquisite murals by Averil Conwell grace the restaurant walls, pictures of the memorable hotel, the outlying buildings and the golf course of earlier days in Lake Placid.

At Frederick's today, you can enjoy a delicious entree with forty-four choices. Among the local favorites are Jumbo Shrimp Scampi, Alaskan King Crab au Gratin, Lemon Sole Oscar, Tournedos Rossinni or one of their famous flaming entrees such as Duckling Grand Marnier or Steak au Poivre. With such a variety of entrees; beef, veal and lamb are all served in dishes guaranteed perfect preparation by the consistency of the

Richards husband-wife team. Dinners come with a soup, a fresh crisp salad and a choice of potato or rice. The helpings are plentiful and enticingly served. The tempting desserts are a la carte and well worth the extra calories.

Come as you are, discover Lake Placid, view the mountain range and enjoy the exquisite food cooked "par excellence" at Frederick's. It is truly a restaurant with high standards that we are all looking for and finding in Lake Placid.

How to get there: *Frederick's is at the north end of Lake Placid village on Signal Hill (just off Rt. 86) Lounge upstairs. Banquet facilities. Dinner. (518) 523-2310.*

While you're there: *A four season resort town. All sports. Hiking. Bicylcing. Attractions. Theater. Shopping. Boat Tours. Four beautiful golf courses nearby. Para-Sailing. Mountain Views. Lakes. Skiing.*

FREDERICK'S SOLE OSCAR

1 6-8 oz. sole filet
2 oz. crabmeat
4 asparagus spears
Salt and pepper

1. Bake sole at 350° oven until it flakes.
2. Top with asparagus spears and sauteed crab.
3. Top with Bearnaise sauce.*

* See glossary

Serves: 1
Preparation: 5 minutes
Cooking: 10-15 minutes

KAHLUA WALNUT ROLL

8 egg whites
8 egg yolks
1-1/2 c. walnuts (finely chopped)
3/4 c. sugar
1 t. baking powder
1 pint heavy cream
1 c. sugar
Pinch of salt
1 shot Kahlua
Powdered sugar

1. Beat egg whites until stiff but not dry.
2. In a separate bowl beat yolks, sugar and salt until pale.
3. Add chopped walnuts and baking powder.
4. Fold egg whites and pour evenly into pan.
5. Bake at 350° for 20 minutes or until cake springs back to the touch on a 12" x 16" baking sheet.
6. Cool cake.
7. Whip cream, Kahlua and sugar.
8. Invert cake onto a towel dusted with powdered sugar.
9. Spread on cream and roll up like a jelly roll.

Serves: 14-15
Preparation: 30 minutes
Cooking: 20 minutes

JIMMY'S 21
EATING AND DRINKING
PLACE

LAKE PLACID

The first visitors to the Lake Placid area were the Iroquois Indians. Later, English soldiers scouted the area during the French and Indian War. Soon the trappers came, one by one, in search of the abundant beaver so well known to the primitive area. By the early 1800's, New Englanders arrived traveling over the old Military Road, the only principal road, to make their settlement in, and near, Lake Placid. By the 1850's a few farmhouses began catering to the Summer visitors and Lake Placid's era as a resort began. Today, this small village provides mountain beauty to both the Summer and Winter visitor, attracting vacationers from all over the world.

For over twenty five years, Jimmy's 21 has played an important part in Lake Placid's progression and among the large variety of eating places. The lakeside view from the small intimate dining room is marvelous; one where you can watch swimmers, rowers, fishermen and boaters-inviting images in the glimmering clean waters of Mirror Lake! In the Winter, the scene changes to a speeding snowmobile or a team of Husky dogs pulling a sled across the stark white ice and snow covered lake. With a backdrop of Whiteface Mountain glistening beyond, it could be a scene in a fairy book fantasy.

Inside, the lounge is located near the front where there is much activity and good humor. It is busy and the mood is happy. It is one of the main meeting places where both resident and visitor gather to exchange a sport story or relax after a day's work. Fast and attentive service in the preparation of food and drink is what invites diners to come back time and time again. The menu is placed before you at precisely the time that you were about to ask for it, and every offering on the bill is so inviting that it is hard to choose. Jimmy's employees take pride in their work and are at all times helpful and courteous-suggesting the best choices of the day.

Jimmy takes pride in the soups that he makes himself, the menu offers one special soup each day. A few years ago, he was the guest on a television show which featured some of his favorites and his secrets of making a good stock base to build a delicious chicken, bean or beef pot of hot soup.

From the menu, you may choose from the char grille, braised meats, veal or seafood and your taste buds will not be disappointed. So, if you are tired of swimming, boating, skiing or skating and just want to relax in a casual and friendly atmosphere, you can dive into a plate of deliciously cooked food, prepared just for you at Jimmy's 21 Eating and Drinking Place.

How to get there: *21 Main Street, Lake Placid. Lunch. Dinner. Lounge. (518) 523-2353.*

While you're there: *Water sports and lake activity. Boat rentals and tours. Snowmobile rentals. Dog sled rides and tobogganing. Power boats are not allowed on Mirror Lake, but Lake Placid is nearby. Public sand beach. Camping permits on State land are required for anyone camping more than three days in one campsite. If you have a group of ten or more a permit is required.*

CHILLED SPANISH GAZPACHO

3 large cucumbers, minced
1-2 t. salt
8 tomatoes, peeled and chopped
2 green peppers, minced
3 green onions, chopped
2 T. vinegar
2 T. olive oil
1 clove garlic, minced
1-1/2 t. sugar
1 pint consomme (beef broth)
2 small cans V-8 juice
Touch of cumin
Salt and pepper to taste
Chopped chives
Croutons

1. Mash cucumber, add 1-2 t. salt and let stand for several minutes.
2. Add chopped tomatoes, green peppers, onions.
3. Mix together vinegar, oil, garlic, sugar, cumin and a touch of salt and pepper. Let stand several minutes.
4. Combine all ingredients: consomme and V-8 juice.
5. CHILL WELL and serve garnished with chives and seasoned croutons.

Serves: 8
Preparation: 30 minutes

CONSOMME BELLEVIEW

1-1/2 quarts chicken broth (well seasoned)
1-1/2 quarts clam juice
1/2 pint heavy cream

1. Combine the broth and clam juice. Bring to a simmer.
2. Whip the heavy cream (until it peaks). Do not add anything to the cream.
3. Using a teaspoon, place a small amount of whipped cream on top.
4. Serve immediately.

Serves: 12 cups
Preparations: 8 minutes
Cooking: 15-20 minutes

VEAL CORDON BLEU

4-5 oz. center cut veal (sliced)
Salt and pepper
Lemon
Granulated garlic
4 oz. ham
4 oz. swiss cheese
4 oz. provolone cheese
Flour
2 eggs
Milk
Bread crumbs
Butter

1. Pound the veal with a mallet to tenderize.
2. Sprinkle each slice with salt, pepper, lemon juice and granulated onion (optional).
3. Slice medium thin 4 ounces of ham, swiss and provolone cheese.
4. Fold over.
5. Carefully blend with flour.
6. Mix egg and milk then dip the veal in batter.
7. Dip in the bread crumbs.
8. Saute in heavy skillet with butter over medium heat. Turn. Takes about 5-6 minutes.
9. Place in 300° oven for 10 minutes, until the cheeses melt slightly.

Serves: 4
Preparation: 20 minutes
Cooking: 16 minutes

BAKED STUFFED BROOK TROUT AMANDINE

1-10-12 oz. brook trout
Salt and pepper
Lemon juice
3 medium shrimp or 2 large shrimp (cooked and chopped)
5 mushrooms (diced)
Butter
2 T. crabmeat
A few almonds (sliced)
Parsley
Lemon slice
Paprika

1. Purchase whole boneless trout.
2. Remove head and tail or have butcher remove it for you.
3. Sprinkle fish with salt and pepper and lemon juice.
4. Set aside.

STUFFING

5. Combine cooked shrimp, sauteed mushrooms, crabmeat, melted butter to bind, chopped parsley, salt and pepper.
6. Mix and place in the cavity of the fish.
7. Lay on a buttered (oil) pan.
8. Sprinkle fish with paprika and melted butter.
9. Bake in oven for 15-20 minutes at 350°.
10. Make an amandine of whole butter melted till slightly colored. Add a few sliced almonds. Cook til beige in color.
11. Pour (ladle) amandine over cooked fish.
12. Garnish with lemon slice and parsley.

Serves: 1
Preparation: 25 minutes
Cooking: 30 minutes

LAKE PLACID HILTON

America has come a long way in the restaurant business in just a short two hundred years. The tremendous growth is mind boggling. Popular restaurants of yesterday, run by industrious and knowledgeable people, many times was a family affair. The husband, good natured and funny, was the host and bartender, the wife prepared the meals and the children attended the dining room as waiter and waitress.

At the Lake Placid Hilton, this tradition has evolved offering a large family within its bounds and, perhaps, the most complete hotel complex north of Albany. Built and opened in August 1979, the complex consists of 178 rooms, 4 swimming pools, beach and boating on Mirror Lake, a 110 seat "Dancing Bear" cocktail lounge and 250 seat dining room plus banquet and meeting rooms to accommodate up to 400 people. This center is an unusual and exciting combination of many activities and American cuisine under one roof, a progressive concept which has caught on all over America.

It has been said that the most important steps in the learning/teaching concept is the attitude of the student and teacher. An attentive student learns much faster with greater results than the disinterested student. Roger Steinbrueck, the executive chef, at the Lake Placid Hilton was just such a student while completing his apprenticeship in Europe. He attended the well-known Cordon Bleu School of Paris until he returned to New York State where he was offered the opportunity as executive chef at the Hilton.

The dinner menu hosts superb entrees prepared under the supervision of Roger. He constantly strives for perfection, artfully preparing the meals. He is especially proud of his Veal and Seafood. Entrees include Veal Cordon Bleu, Shrimp Scampi, Wiener Schnitzel, Fillet of Sole, Sirloin Steak, and Chateaubriand for Two.

Every Sunday morning the dining room opens its doors where an extravaganza of feasting unfolds. The Sunday Brunch is a spectacular event of gastronomical delights. Surrounded by selections of Eggs Benedict, Roast Beef, Crisp Bacon, Baked Ham, Roasted Link Sausage and Imported Salami, Assorted cold Sliced Meats, Lasagne, Fresh Fruits and Salads, the delectable dishes are outrageous. Don't forget to leave room for the Deluxe Viennese Party Table. Arlie Adams, the pastry chef, has included her recipes in this book for you to enjoy. Sunday vacationers would do well to plan around this weekly event.

The North Country is fortunate to have a hotel whose hospitality is able to reach out to everyone, to offer such a tremendous variety, and still maintain a feeling of informality with intimate corners in its large capacity.

How to get there: *1 Mirror Lake Drive (on the Main St.) Breakfast. Lunch. Dinner. Rooms. Swimming Pools. Lounge. Entertainment. (518) 523-4411.*

While you're there: *Lake Placid offers a vast assortment of museums, sporting events, attractions, performing arts, tournaments and scenic vistas that make it a four season vacationland. Windsurfing. Boating. Sailing. Swimming. Fishing. There are forty-six major Adirondack peaks over 4,000 feet high. Most of them have trails leading to the summits. "Herd trails" may be found on the trailless mountains.*

SOUR CREAM COFFEE CAKE

3/4 c. butter, soft
1-1/2 c. sugar
3 eggs
1-1/2 t. vanilla
3 c. flour
1-1/2 t. baking powder
1-1/2 t. baking soda
1/4 t. salt
1-1/2 c. sour cream

FILLING

1 lb. brown sugar
1 T. cinnamon
1/2 c. walnuts, chopped
1/2 c. dry cake crumbs

1. Cream butter, sugar, eggs and vanilla until light and creamy.
2. Add one half of the flour with remaining dry ingredients.
3. Add sour cream, then remaining flour and mix until smooth.
4. Place one-half of the batter in pan.
5. Sprinkle with sugar-cinnamon mixture.
6. Add remaining batter and sprinkle top with more sugar-cinnamon mixture.

Makes: 2 loaf pans
Preparation: 30 minutes
Cooking: 50-60 minutes at 350°

CHOCOLATE WALNUT TORTE

5 oz. semi-sweet chocolate
1-1/2 c. walnuts, ground
2 T. granulated sugar
2 T. all purpose flour
3/4 c. butter soft
1/2 c. granulated sugar
5 egg yolks
5 egg whites

1. Melt chocolate and set aside.
2. Mix walnuts and 2 tablespoons of flour together.
3. In large bowl, cream butter, add 1/2 cup of sugar. Beat until light.
4. Add egg yolks, one at a time, beating well after each. Stir in chocolate, then add to nut mixture.
5. In large mixing bowl, beat egg whites until stiff. Fold egg whites into chocolate batter.
6. Spoon into 9" springform pan (greased).
7. Bake at 350° for 40 minutes.

Serves: 8-10
Preparation: 30 minutes
Cooking: 40 minutes

HILTON BREAKFAST ROLLS

1/3 c. shortening
1/2 c. granulated sugar
1 egg
1-1/2 c. flour
1-1/2 t. baking powder
1/2 t. salt
1/4 t. nutmeg
1/2 c. milk
1/2 c. sugar
1 t. cinnamon
1/2 c. dry cake crumbs
1/2 c. butter, melted

1. Beat shortening, sugar and egg until light and lemon color.
2. Add dry ingredients alternating with milk.
3. Spoon into greased muffin tins, three fourths full.
4. Bake at 350° for 20-25 minutes.
5. Mix sugar, cinnamon, cake crumbs. Roll warm muffins in butter, then into sugar mixture.

Serves: 12 (1 dozen muffins)
Preparation: 15 minutes
Cooking: 20-25 minutes

108

MIRROR LAKE INN

LAKE PLACID

Mirror Lake Inn is a restaurant with an award winning history of its own. Back in 1924, Climena Alford and William Wikoff were married and moved to Massachusetts where Mr. Wikoff invented the concept of the "Fuller Brush Man" and quickly became a financial success.

Two years later the couple moved back to Lake Placid where they created many firsts for the community. At this same time, two of three estates stood where Mirror Lake Inn is now situated. They converted one of the estates into an attractive resort named Mir-a-Lac-Inn. In preparation for the 1932 Olympics, they had built a dining room and winterized the Inn for the Norwegian Olympic team's stay. During those Olympics, the Europeans introduced and demonstrated downhill skiing, hoping to include this exciting sport in the future Olympics. Six years later the first electric powered rope tow was set in motion on "Dream Hill" (the slope directly behind the Inn.) Another first took place about 1946 when the Wikoff's purchased a snowmaking machine and artificial snow was made to ensure the proper skiing conditions on Dream Hill. Mirror Lake Inn, too, can tell of the first bobsled run which came down Dream Hill over the road and hit the ice of Mirror Lake.

The Inn, always, has been known, first, for its gracious dining and delicious food due to the care which went into every menu item. Overlooking Mirror Lake, the dining room is very elegant. Candlelit tables are dressed in white linen and colorful fresh flowers. On the walls of the room are a very charming series of oil paintings representing typical scenes of Lake Placid in its earlier days. These were completed by Averil Courtney Conwell, a nationally recognized artist who is now living in Lake Placid.

For sixteen years under the direction of Herb Rock, the executive chef, the kitchen prepares only the finest food obtainable. Lightly seasoned sauces compliment the delicate flavor of meats, seafoods and vegetables. Breads are baked daily in their bakeshop using time tested recipes that have become a Mirror Lake tradition. Herb, who really looks like a chef, jokes about cooking for "one hundred years," but credits his Mother who started teaching him at fourteen years old. Herb never tires of his efforts to bring the best cuisine to the Adirondacks.

Today, the Inn is owned by the Weibrecht family who continue to foster gracious living in a family atmosphere. Probably the most singularly important aspect of the Inn, both historically and presently, is that the guests and staff are happy to be there and that's what good living is all about. Enjoy the Mirror Lake Inn as a part of the history of Lake Placid and a part of the Adirondack adventure of fine cuisine.

How to get there: *5 Mirror Lake Drive. Lake Placid. Lakeview lunch and dinner. Two cocktail lounges. Rooms. Boating. Tennis. Private Beach. (518) 523-2544.*

While you're there: *Skiing. Skating. Para Sailing rides are offered directly in front of the Inn. Dog sled rides. Museums. Attractions. Theater. Watersports. Strenuous hiking and easy walking trails. Festivals throughout the year. There are guided boat tours-hour long cruises covering miles of Adirondack beauty.*

FRENCH ONION SOUP

5-1/2 c. onions
3 T. butter
1/4 t. sugar
1/2 c. dry sherry
1 quart beef stock
Salt
Pepper
French bread (4 slices)
Provolone cheese (4 slices)

1. Thinly slice the onions.
2. Sauté the onions in soup pot with butter until brown.
3. Add 1/4 t. sugar.
4. Add 1 quart of beef stock.
5. Add salt, pepper and sherry.
6. Cut french bread in rounds.
7. Top with provolone cheese.
8. Put under broiler until cheese begins to brown.

BEEF STOCK

Water
2 T. beef base or 2 bouillion cubes

Serves: 2
Preparation: 20 minutes
Cooking: 35 minutes

SALAD NICOISE

1 head of lettuce
2 endive or chicory
2 T. black olives
6 cherry tomatoes
French dressing
Parmesan cheese

1. Core head of lettuce.
2. Wash and drain thoroughly 1 head of lettuce.
3. Tear into bite size pieces.
4. Tear endive for salad bowl.
5. Chop and pit olives.
6. Scald, skin and quarter cherry tomatoes.
7. Add to salad with French dressing.
8. Dust with cheese.

Serves: 6-8
Preparation: 10 minutes

CRABMEAT LORENZO

1 T. butter
1 T. flour
1/2 c. milk
1/2 T. Dijon mustard
1/2 T. worcestershire sauce
Salt and Pepper
1/2 c. crabmeat
Swiss cheese (grated)
Toast rounds
Parsley

1. Make cream sauce of 1 T. butter, 1 T. flour.
2. Add 1/2 c. milk.
3. Season with 1/2 T. Dijon mustard.
4. Add 1/2 T. worcestershire sauce.
5. Add salt and pepper and 1/2 c. crabmeat.
6. Sprinkle with grated Swiss cheese.
7. Spread on buttered toast rounds.
8. Broil to light brown.
9. Sprinkle with parsley.

Serves: 1
Preparation: 20 minutes

ANNA POTATOES

1 potato
1 T. butter
Salt and pepper
1/2 c. chicken stock
Parmesan cheese
Paprika

1. Line a casserole with a sliced raw potato.
2. Dot with butter.
3. Salt and pepper to taste.
4. Add 1/2 c. chicken stock to bottom of casserole.
5. Top with parmesan cheese seasoned with a little paprika.
6. Cover tightly and bake 350° for 1 hour.
7. Remove cover and brown until done.

Serves: 1
Preparation: 5 minutes
Cooking: 1 hour

RASPBERRY PIE

1 quart raspberries
1 T. cornstarch
1-2 T. butter

1. Thaw and drain frozen raspberries. Save juice.
2. Mix 1 T. cornstarch with 1 T. water.
3. Heat juice to boiling and slowly add cornstarch mixture.
4. When sauce becomes thick, add 1/3 c. sugar.
5. Fill 9" pie shell with berries and sauce.
6. Dot with butter.
7. Bake in preheated 400° oven.
8. Immediately lower heat to 350°.
9. When juice bubbles and pie is brown, remove from oven.

PIE CRUST

2 c. all purpose flour
1/3 c. lard
1/3 c. butter
1 t. salt
1/4 c. water

1. Beat all the ingredients with electric mixer.
2. Cool in refrigerator.
3. Roll out for pie shell.

Serves: 6
Preparation: 20 minutes
Cooking: 10 minutes/45 minutes

CRABMEAT AU GRATIN

2 T. butter
4 c. Alaskan king crab
1-1/2 T. flour
Pinch of salt and pepper
1/2 pint of milk
Worcestershire sauce
Parmesan cheese
Paprika

1. Melt 2 T. of butter in pan.
2. Sautē the crabmeat.
3. Add flour, salt and pepper.
4. Add 1/2 pint of milk and a dash of worcestershire sauce.
5. Stir until slightly thickened.
6. Place in casserole dish and top with grated parmesan cheese and ,paprika.
7. Heat in 300° oven for 10 minutes or broil until brown.

Serves: 4
Preparation: 20 minutes

ADIRONDACK HOTEL
ON LONG LAKE

True to its name, Long Lake is a narrow fifteen mile long body of water flowing northeasterly through the heart of the Adirondack Park. Those faithful to the sleepy village of Long Lake say the famous Adirondack guideboat first cut the water on this very same lake. Today, you can still see the guideboats "Sunday touring" in front of the Adirondack Hotel. The Hotel stands at the end of the lake and holds a special appeal for "the ourdoorsman" in everyone.

Resident owners, Bob and Marijane Lucci with their warm hospitality, create an "at home" atmosphere. They offer only the freshest meats and seafood served in the true Adirondack tradition. Delicious!

The Adirondack Hotel traces its history back to the 1800's and is now one of the oldest active hotels in the Adirondacks. It claims only six past owners. Bob and Marijane have given the last ten years in time and energy refurbishing the hotel with depictions of Adirondack wildlife. Some of the most outstanding treasures were acquired from previous owners of the hotel. They are proud of the full size black bear which is one of the principals of the hotel's decor. Many local hunters attest to the fact that it is the second largest bear ever captured in the Park. Another interesting collectors' charm is the large moosehead which was purchased from the "Hunter" collection. Hunter was a famous tennis pro in the '30's and 40's. A twenty-two point deer, mounted on an antique mirror, comes from the Clement collection. Clement, a former hotel

119

owner, was highly acclaimed for the food and service, as are the Luccis today.

The Adirondack Hotel on Long Lake attracts people from as far away as New York City. They enjoy the well known feasts and rural lakeside surroundings.

It has been said that Long Lake, with its well known guideboat, belongs to the mixed evergreen and hardwood forest and the dancing waters of the lakes, rivers and ponds. You, too, can relive this experience by dining at the Adirondack wilderness. Come as you are and enjoy the picturesque waterfront setting. The hotel's atmosphere is casual and friendly offering delicious lake dining.

How to get there: 1 Lake St., Long Lake. (518) 624-4700. Located on Routes 30 and 28. Open late Spring and closes early Fall. Everyday from July 1 to September 1. Breakfast. Lunch. Dinner. Rooms. Cottages.

While you're there: The Adirondack Museum is located, not far, at Blue Mountain Lake. The best museum for depicting Adirondack history. Hiking—(Northville-Lake Placid trail.) Canoes may be rented in Long Lake at the marinas. Boating. Trout fishing. Seaplane rides.

CHICKEN PARISIENNE

2-4 whole chicken breasts, halved
Salt and pepper to taste
3 T. butter or margarine
1 small onion
1 c. sour cream
1 c. fresh mushrooms, sliced
1/2 pint half and half
1/2-3/4 c. sherry

1. Season breasts with salt and pepper. Melt butter in a skillet.
2. Brown chicken on both sides.
3. Arrange chicken, onion and mushrooms in a casserole or baking pan.
4. Mix remaining ingredients together in a separate dish. Pour over chicken.
5. Bake in 400° oven for 40-50 minutes.

Serves: 4
Preparation: 15 minutes
Cooking: 40-50 minutes

DUCKLING SEVILLE

2 ducklings (4 to 5 pounds each) quartered
1 c. bitter orange marmalade
2 T. Cointreau liqueur

1. Have ducklings quartered at market. Place skin side up in shallow roasting pan. Roast at 325° for 2-1/2 to 3 hours or until tender.
2. Meanwhile combine marmalade and Cointreau.
3. Twenty minutes before roasting time is up baste ducklings with this mixture and finish roasting.
4. Serve surrounded with border of cooked wild and long grain rice.
5. Garnish with an orange.

NOTE: It is best using bittersweet marmalade imported from England.

Serves: 4-8
Preparation: 7 minutes
Cooking: 2-1/2 to 3 hours

CALORIE CONSCIOUS CHEESECAKE

1/4 c. butter
1 egg yolk
1 c. sifted flour
2 T. cold water
2-2/3 c. whole milk yogurt (21 oz.)
2-2/3 c. low fat cottage cheese (21 oz.)
8 large eggs
1-2/3 c. sugar
1 t. vanilla
1/2 c. flour

1. Cut butter with egg yolk and mix into 1 c. flour and add water to form dough.
2. Roll out about one third of the dough and fit on bottom of greased 9" springform pan. Trim to fit.
3. Bake at 400° for 10 minutes or until golden. Cool.
4. Grease sides of pan and fit over base. Roll out remaining dough and line side of pan.
5. Whirl yogurt and cheese, half at a time, in blender until smooth.
6. Beat together eggs, sugar, vanilla and one half cup flour. Stir in yogurt mixture.
7. Pour into crust and bake 475° for 10 minutes. Lower heat to 250° and bake about one hour or until custard is set. Cool on rack. Refrigerate overnight.

NOTE: You can top with fruit or fruit glaze if you prefer.

Serves: 16
Preparation: 20 minutes
Cooking: 1 hour 20 minutes

LUCCIS OF LONG LAKE
LINDY CHEESECAKE

1/2 c. fine crumbs
Butter
2 limes
1 orange
1-1/2 lbs. cream cheese
1 t. vanilla
1/2 c. heavy cream
3/4 c. 2 T. sugar
4 large eggs
2 T. sour cream
1/4 c. half and half

1. Preheat oven to 375°. Butter a round cake pan (8" x 2").
2. Sprinkle inside with crumbs, shake off excess.
3. Grate limes and orange. Set aside gratings.
4. Add cream cheese to mixing bowl. Add grated rinds and vanilla, beating.
5. Gradually add the heavy cream and sugar, beating constantly on moderate speed.
6. Add the eggs, one at a time, beating well after each addition.
7. Beat in the sour cream and half and half.
8. Pour into the prepared pan and smooth the top. Set the pan in a larger pan and pour boiling water around it.
9. Place in the oven and bake one and one quarter hours until the center is set. Remove from water and let stand on rack for 10 minutes.
10. Invert and unmold while hot. Let stand until cool.

Serves: 12
Preparation: 25 minutes
Cooking: 1 hour and 25 minutes

ADIRONDACK VEAL GOURMET

12 very thin slices of fresh veal
Flour for dredging
Salt and pepper to taste
2 T. butter
1 t. shallots
1 pint heavy cream
2 c. fresh mushrooms, sliced
4 T. white seedless grapes

1. Dredge veal with seasoned flour. Heat butter in skillet, add the veal and brown a few minutes on both sides until meat is fork tender.
2. Remove the veal to a serving dish and keep warm.
3. Add shallots to the skillet and simmer for 1 minute.
4. Add heavy cream and the mushrooms and grapes.
5. Bring to a boil and cook for two minutes.
6. Pour over veal and serve.

Servings: 4
Preparation: 5 minutes
Cooking: 9 minutes

CASA DEL SOL

CASA DEL SOL

SARANAC LAKE

The residents of Saranac Lake and Lake Placid will tell you without even being asked that the Casa Del Sol Restaurant is not only their pride and joy, but the most authentic Mexican restaurant in the Adirondacks. And, that is not hard to believe after spending a wintry evening, dining at the Casa Del Sol when most people would prefer to spend the evening at home.

The "South of the Border" atmosphere is captured to perfection in this small friendly Mexican restaurant on Route 86 in Saranac Lake, just ten minutes to Lake Placid.

It is very clear that Harry Tucker, owner since 1978, has discovered the gold across the border. This airy, cozy restaurant with its desert, tropical decor offers a full range of Mexican dishes not easily found in the Adirondack area. The Margaritas are super and served in oversized glasses. They are large enough to be what one would consider two drinks and available in colors-white or green.

To ward off the evening's cold, we began with a delicious soup. Next, we shared a light snack of nachos. These crispy, light fried chips are served dripping with hot Monterey Jack cheese and mildly hot jalepeno peppers. For an entree, try the hearty flautas- two crispy, fried corn tortillas wrapped together with a pork filling and sauce, topped with sour cream, lettuce and tomatoes. Each choice has a distinctive flavor and very attractively served. An irresistable dessert is their homemade chocolate cheesecake.

The service is consistently superior. The eager waitress is both helpful and friendly, especially if you are unfamiliar with Mexican foods.

The Casa Del Sol is certainly not expensive. It is a definite triumph when one yields to Mexican cuisine.

Casa Del Sol--We salute you!

How to get there: *Casa Del Sol is located at 154 Flower Ave. (Route 86) between Saranac Lake and Lake Placid. Open from noon until 10 P.M. Monday through Saturday. Sundays from 5 P.M. until 10 P.M. No credit cards. (518) 891-0977.*

While you're there: *85% of the housing units in Saranac Lake were built prior to 1940, when Saranac Lake was a major health center. One such place is the Robert Lewis Stevenson cottage, now a museum and open to the public. Today Saranac Lake is known to be a unique out-of-the-way spot for vacations with many events; art shows, flea markets, craft shows and an annual antique show is held every summer. It is filled with interesting shops. Throughout July and August an annual Festival of Music is held at different locations in Saranac Lake and Lake Placid. Fishing. Boating. Hiking. Summer and Winter community events.*

BLOODY MARIA

1-1/2 oz. tequila
3 oz. tomato juice
1 dash lime juice
1/2 t. worcestershire sauce
2 or 3 drops tabasco sauce
Salt and pepper to taste
A lime wedge

1. Shake with ice and strain into glass over ice cubes.
2. Garnish with a lime wedge.

Serves: 1

NOTES

CHIMICHANGAS

2 flour torillas
3/4 c. chicken, cooked
1/4 c. onions, cut up
1/4 c. green peppers, cut up
1/2 c. cheese, grated
Lettuce (for garnish), chopped
Tomatoes, diced, (for garnish)
Cheese, shredded (for garnish)

1. Roll a flour tortilla around a mixture of chicken, onions, green peppers and cheese.
2. Make sure ends are folded in to prevent spillage.
3. Deep fry until golden brown.
4. Garnish top with chopped lettuce, diced tomatoes and shredded cheese.

Serves: 1
Preparation: 15 minutes
Cooking: 4-5 minutes

NOTES

NACHOS

3 corn tortillas
12 jalapeno pepper rings
12 oz. Monterey Jack cheese, shredded
1 c. lettuce, shredded
1 tomato, cut in small pieces

1. Quarter corn tortillas and deep fry for 1-2 minutes.
2. Arrange on a platter placing jalapeno pepper rings on each chip.
3. Cover chips with shredded cheese.
4. Place under broiler until cheese is golden brown.
5. Garnish with lettuce and tomato.

Serves: 2
Preparation: 5 minutes
Cooking: 1-2 minutes/2 minutes

NOTES

The
Hotel Saranac
of Paul Smith's College

THE HOTEL SARANAC OF PAUL SMITH'S COLLEGE

SARANAC LAKE

"Something old, something new, something borrowed and something blue" may have been originally written for a bride but it also describes The Hotel Saranac in the Village of Saranac Lake in Franklin County. The Hotel, built in 1927 on the site of several former schools, (something old) is a full service commercial hotel owned and operated by Paul Smith's College for training hotel and restaurant management students. Under professional supervision, the students are assigned to all positions in the hotel from busperson to maitre d', from pantry person to chef, from desk clerk to student manager (always something new). Operating 365 days a year in the popular resort town, ninety-two all newly refurbished room hotel gives students practical experience so highly valued in the hospitality industry.

The dining room, decorated in light soft-colored wood with blue carpeting and upholstered chairs (something blue), offers a wide selection; plain and fancy sandwiches, fourteen dinner entrees and gourmet masterpieces. The students are continually testing their gourmet fantasies: first in the kitchen and then on the patrons-- constantly searching for the total perfection they strive for. You will find that their recipes made from scratch are every bit as good as "Mothers."

Every Thursday evening a popular and successful buffet is prepared and served to the guests. The menu is planned with a theme highlighting food from another country (something borrowed). From the many choices, beginning with three or four appetizers and ending with as many tempting desserts, you can eat as much as you like. It is an event! The students deserve mounds of applause for offering this special occasion to both residents and visitors.

In the age of fast food and sprawling hotel chains, you will be pleased to know there is still a place where traditional Adirondack hospitality remains. The Hotel Saranac is a place where good food and drink, personal service and comfortable rooms are still reasonably priced. Everyone should experience this special Hotel which has enjoyed a fine reputation for over fifty years and Saranac Lake, one of the most beautiful areas in New York State. On your visit to the hotel, ask to meet some of the future cooks in the regal atmosphere that prepares them so expertly that they could cook for the kings and queens of the world.

How to get there: The Hotel Saranac is located in the center of the Village of Saranac Lake. 101 Main St. Breakfast. Lunch. Dinner. Cocktail Lounge. Bakery. Rooms. (518) 891-2200.

While you're there: The Hotel is surrounded by many lakes and acres of Adirondack wilderness. Minutes to the shores of Lake Flower. Water sports. Sightseeing attractions. Golfing. Fishing. Hiking. Performing Arts. Skiing. Tennis. Snowmobiling. Snowshoeing. The shops and businesses of the community are just out the front door of the Hotel.

GLAZED CARROTS

1 lb. carrots, sliced
3 oz. butter
2 oz. sugar
1/8 lemon
Salt

1. Blanche carrots until tender but firm.
2. Heat butter and add carrots.
3. Add sugar and toss.
4. Season to taste.

Serves: 4
Preparation: 20 minutes

NOTES

CHICKEN SARANAC

6-8 oz. boneless chicken breast
12 oz. chicken veloute (reduced chicken stock)
6 oz. heavy cream
6 oz. Reisling wine
1 T. shallots
Salt and Pepper
2 oz. butter
Flour

1. Remove skin from breasts.
2. Lightly flour breasts and saute until golden brown.
3. Deglaze with wine. Add shallots, veloute* and cream. Reduce to thickness of gravy.
4. Simmer slowly until chicken is done.
5. Salt and pepper to taste.

NOTE: Serve over noodles or rice.
* See glossary

Serves: 6
Preparation: 10 minutes
Cooking: 45 minutes

GERMAN CHEESE BEER SOUP

2 gallons rich chicken broth
1 quart heavy cream
1 quart of beer
1 lb. butter
1 lb. flour
4 lbs. aged cheddar cheese
2 T. worcestershire sauce
1 t. tabasco sauce
1/2 t. dried mustard
Salt
Parsley
Pepper
Pretzels

1. Heat chicken stock to a simmer.
2. In a heavy pot, melt butter and add flour. Cook for a few minutes.
3. Add stock to roux. Be careful so it does not boil over.
4. Add thinly sliced cheese and simmer until cheese is melted.
5. Add beer.
6. Add cream and season just before serving.
7. Garnish with a pretzel and chopped parsley.

Serves: 50
Preparation: 45 minutes

NOTE: We have not reduced this recipe from the original. By using the exact recipe, you will achieve the perfect results as experienced at The Saranac. Make this full recipe and always have the soup on hand or have a group of friends in to enjoy it with you!

RICE PILAF

1 quart rice
1 quart chicken stock
1 large onion, finely diced
4 bay leaves
1/4 lb. butter

1. Saute onion in butter.
2. Add rice and stir until all is coated with butter.
3. Add hot stock and bay leaves. Heat to a simmer.
4. Cover and bake in 375° oven for 25-30 minutes.

Serves: 20
Preparation: 10 minutes
Cooking: 30 minutes

THE HOHMEYER FAMILY
presents

The Lodge

"A Rare Dining Experience"

THE LODGE

LAKE CLEAR

The Lodge is a rustic Old World Inn located in the heart of the Northern Adirondacks. Surrounded by glorious mountains and countless bodies of water, The Lodge is located on the narrow forest pined Route 30 on Lake Clear. It is a peak dining experience quite different from the other restaurants in the book. As no formal advertising has ever been undertaken since their inception twenty years ago, this restaurant relies on word of mouth of the high standards of dining offered by the Hohmeyer family. Residents will tell you, not only, that it's their pride and joy, but also, a most unique Adirondack dining experience. The secret ingredient is the superior quality of Mrs. Hohmeyer's cooking. The intimate Lodge specializes in German culinary delights. It operates by reservation only, which is limited to forty guests and one seating each evening from six o'clock to nine o'clock.

As you arrive, Mr. Hohmeyer welcomes and escorts your party to the large fireplaced rumpus room. Here you may enjoy a coctail as a prelude offering to the meal of the evening. There is no a la carte. Each complete meal includes an appetizer, salad, a bowl of "stock started" soup, the main entree, dessert and coffee.

Elsbeth Hohmeyer prepares the full course meals entirely by herself on an old fashioned stove in the traditional home cooked European manner. She uses no recipes, but the specialties have been in her family nearly forever. In fact, her recipes on the following pages had to be written out especially for this book. She cooks from taste and memory. Given free reign in the kitchen, she prepares such entrees as Wienerschnitzel, Roast Pork, Sauerbraten, Roast Beef, Potato Dumplings and Red Cabbage, plus many other selections--do come with a hearty appetite!

End the evening with one of the three desserts that she has made that very day and there you have it--an evening in Lake Clear in the Adirondacks.

It would be worth arranging your vacation time to include this small restaurant, for it has certainly earned the distinctive reputation of excellence.

If you wish to stay longer and enjoy the friendly, homelike atmosphere on the lake, they do offer a few rooms and a cottage. You can relax under the pines, enjoy the view and lake breezes, or swim at their private beach on Lake Clear.

How to get there: *On Route 30 at Lake Clear. About 8 miles from Saranac Lake. Dinner with reservation only. Cottage. Rooms. Open May 1. (518) 891-1489.*

While you're there: *Golfing at Saranac Inn is 3 miles. Tours of Topridge (Marjorie Meriweather Post's summer home) is just 6 miles. Saranac Lake has shopping. Mountain hiking. Horseback riding. Boating. Fishing. Camping. For a summer outing St. Regis "The Seven Carries" is a most beautiful place for canoeing. It includes 10 ponds and, of course, 7 carries. From Plattsburgh, take Route 3 toward Saranac Lake. Turn right to Onchiota and left at Onchiota following the signs to Paul Smith's College. The canoe map at Paul Smith's College boat dock clearly shows the area. The longest carry is .6 miles. Bring your camera as Bog Pond has millions of wildflowers blooming that you will want to capture on film.*

POTATO DUMPLINGS

3 eggs
3 lb. potatoes
1/2 c. flour
4 T. cornstarch
Salt and pepper to taste
Nutmeg to taste

1. Boil, peel, and mash potatoes.
2. Mix all the ingredients with your hands. If batter sticks to your hands, add more flour.
3. Roll into balls the size of golf balls. Set aside.
4. Before dinner, drop the balls into a large pot of boiling water.
5. Lower heat to simmer. Do not cover.
6. When dumplings begin to swim, they are finished.
7. Take out with slotted spoon.
8. Pour sauce from Sauerbraten over dumplings.

Serves: 6-8
Preparation: 15 minutes
Cooking: 12-25 minutes

SAUERBRATEN

6 lb. eye of the round roast
1 T. salt
1 T. sugar
12 peppercorns
1 huge onion, sliced
7 cloves
5 bay leaves
2 stalks celery, cut up
2 carrots, cut up
1/2 c. vinegar
1/2 c. red wine
1 c. boiling water

1. Add meat and all the ingredients to a large glass or pottery bowl.
2. Stir thoroughly and set in refrigerator for five days.
3. Turn meat over twice a day with wooden spoon.

AFTER 5 DAYS

1 onion, sliced
2 stalks celery, sliced
2 carrots, cut up
Tomato paste
3 slices of bacon
Red wine

4. After 5 days, take meat out of the liquid. Throw liquid away.
5. In roasting pan, brown 3 strips of bacon with meat.
6. Add onion, celery, carrots and a large spoonful of tomato paste.
7. Continue browning. Add water for moisture, but do not cover.
8. Roast in oven at 350° for 3-3 1/2 hours or until tender. Continue adding water for moisture, while in the oven.

continued on next page

9. Take out meat and drain liquid.
10. If needed, mix a little flour with the red wine to make sauce.
11. When serving, slice very thin.

NOTE: Great served with red cabbage and potato dumplings.

Serves: 6-8
Preparation: 20 minutes/25 minutes
Cooking: 3-3 1/2 hours

NOTES

RED CABBAGE

6 T. bacon fat
2 T. vinegar
1 medium red cabbage
4 small sweet-sour apples, sliced
1 onion, chopped
4 cloves
2-1/2 T. sugar
Salt and pepper to taste

1. Brown ingredients before putting in cabbage.
2. Cook very slow.
3. For better taste, add red wine (very little).

Serves: 5-6
Preparation: 25 minutes

RED FOX RESTAURANT

Franklin County, with its fertile soil, unmatched forests, abundant lakes and mountains drew early settlers across Lake Champlain. With the growth of the logging business and the influx of people arriving to the area for its clear, clean mountain air came the birth of Saranac Lake. Nestled in the high peaks of the Adirondack Mountains it became known as a health center. With its clean air, along with limited exercise, proper diet and peace, Saranac Lake became the promise of health for many people. Today, more for the benefit of the human mind, its appeal continues to call sportsmen, nature lovers and tourists year round.

The Red Fox Restaurant also attracts year round visitors and residents and, no wonder! The Red Fox is a delightful restaurant full of aromatic fragrances. The comfortable cocktail lounge and fireplace sittings allows you time to enjoy the relaxed atmosphere or engage in conversations of the day's activities before dinner.

A refreshing and pleasing touch is the large selection on the menu with three evening specialties-healthy portions of prime rib, a seafood brochette on a bed of seasoned rice and fresh fish bathed in a delicious cheese sauce. Hot homemade bread, soup, salad and potato are included with every meal.

The exceptional quality of the food is no accident at the Red Fox Restaurant. It is the result of years of intense interest and dedication in the art of food preparation. Harriet and Bill Walasky have spent many years perfecting each recipe with meticulous care through study and early training.

For dessert, try one of their oversized slices of cheesecake, or for

143

chocolate lovers, the delicate chocolate mousse.

Let the winning combination of Saranac Lake and the Red Fox Restaurant entertain you. You can count on a thoroughly good time!

How to get there: *Leave the Village of Saranac Lake on Route 3 West, go three miles and it is on your left. Cocktail Lounge. Dinner. (518) 891-2127.*

While you're there: *Canoeing. Hiking. Downhill and cross-country skiing. Snowmobiling. The last week in January, International dog sled races are held in Saranac Lake. In February, the village celebrates the oldest Winter Carnival in the United States. Summer includes Guideboat and Canoe races, an annual Antique show and a Paint and Pallet Festival.*

CHICKEN ALASKA

4-8 oz. boneless chicken breasts
8 oz. Alaskan king crabmeat
1 bunch broccoli tops
4 oz. butter (solid)
2 T. shallots, chopped
2 cloves garlic, chopped
White pepper
1/4 c. Rhine wine
1 lemon
Basil
Parsley, chopped and fresh

1. Lay chicken breast skin down and lightly score.
2. Place 1 oz. of butter on each chicken breast.
3. Lightly sprinkle wine and follow with dusting of shallots, garlic; white pepper, juice of the lemon, basil and parsley.
4. Follow with 2 oz. of crabmeat per breast and divide the broccoli tops evenly.
5. Neatly fold tightly stuffed breast.
6. Bake in 350° oven for 50 minutes or until the doneness is reached depending on oven temperature in your home.
7. Top with cheddar cheese sauce.*
8. Garnish with parsley flowers and peach half.
* See following recipe page.

Serves: 4
Preparation: 10 minutes
Cooking: 50 minutes

CHEDDAR CHEESE SAUCE

1 pint light cream
1-1/2 c. sharp cheese, shredded
1/2 c. chicken stock
White pepper to taste
Tabasco to taste
Celery powder to taste
Chopped parsley to taste
1/4 c. sherry wine
2 T. Chablis wine
Butter Roux*

1. In saucepan add cream, chicken stock, wine, white pepper, celery powder and parsley.
2. Bring to a light boil. Add roux thickened to desired consistency.
3. Add cheddar cheese. Whip until smooth. Follow with sherry and tabasco to taste.

* See glossary

Serves: 4
Preparation: 10 minutes

BEEF BROCHETTE

4-12" skewers
12-1 1/2" sirloin steaks, cubed
8 red onion wedges
4 green pepper wedges
8 mushroom caps, medium
8 oz. butter
Chablis wine
Teriyaki sauce

1. Starting with red onion, beef, mushroom cap, beef, tomato, green pepper, beef, mushroom cap, beef, red onion put on skewers and place on a sheet pan.
2. Place equal amounts of butter over each skewer and put under broiler. Broil until vegetables are tender and desired doneness of meat is met. Turn once.
3. Sprinkle equal amounts of teriyaki sauce and Chablis wine combining with melted butter and meat juices.
4. Serve over Rice Pilaf, placing remaining sauce over each.
5. Garnish with chopped parsely, parsely flakes and spiced apple.

Serves: 4
Preparation: 20 minutes
Cooking: Until desired doneness.

HALIBUT BELLAVISTA

4-8 to 10 oz. Halibut steaks
1 large tomato
1 green pepper
1 large onion (red)
1 lemon
Chablis wine to taste
Basil to taste
Celery seed to taste
Onion powder to taste
Garlic powder
Romano cheese
White pepper
3-4 oz. butter patties

1. Place steaks on lightly oiled casserole or small sheet pan.
2. Sprinkle evenly the juice of lemon and an equal amount of white wine.
3. Lightly dust, to taste, with remaining spices.
4. Slice the tomato, peppers and onions.
5. First place the onions, then peppers, then tomatoes over the fish.
6. Follow with 2 oz. melted butter on the ingredients.
7. Lighly sprinkle with cheese.
8. Bake in 400° oven until flaky and tender, about 15 minutes.
9. Serve with remaining butter and herbs reserved in the cooking pan. Pour over steaks.
10. Garnish with lemon and parsley flower.

Serves: 4
Preparation: 10 minutes
Cooking: 15 minutes

RICE PILAF

2 c. brown rice
5-6 c. chicken stock
1/2 c. green pepper
1 c. Spanish onion
1 c. celery
1/2 c. mushrooms
Garlic powder to taste
White pepper to taste
Sweet basil to taste
1/4 c. Chablis wine

1. Bring stock to boil, add rice. Cook 30 minutes. Set aside.
2. Melt butter in saucepan. Combine pepper, onion, celery and mushrooms.
3. Add herbs and spices. Saute until tender.
4. Add Chablis wine to taste and then rice.

NOTE: Very good served with Beef Brochette.

Serves: 4
Preparation: 15 minutes
Cooking: 30 minutes

The
ALGONQUIN

Restaurant

THE ALGONQUIN RESTAURANT

BOLTON LANDING

The Algonquin is a dock-side restaurant with a spectacular view of Lake George--a century old "legend in its own time." Located in Bolton Landing, nine miles from Lake George Village, it first opened in 1847 as a tea room for the guests of the Algonquin Hotel. The Hotel was located across the highway until, in 1959, the run down hotel burned. Helen and Harris Smith then bought the tea room and ran it successfully as a popular "mom and pop" operation. This popularity of the tea room prompted remodeling in 1964.

It was, and still is, the home of their son, Teddy Smith and his wife, Patsy, who continue the family traditions passed to them from his parents. Where once Harris greeted his guests, Teddy and Patsy now make everyone feel welcome. Because of continued success another major and more extensive expansion was undertaken in 1978. The Algonquin now boasts of two separate dining rooms which offer guests a choice of dining formally "Topside" or more casually downstairs in the "Pub Room."

The Topside dining room's gourmet offerings include appetizers and entrees in which you can easily enjoy a delicious, satisfying evening. The flavorful food melts in your mouth. The attractive, crisp salad and freshly baked rolls are worthy of top note, too. An attentive captain, professional, but friendly waiters, and a fluctuating vista of Lake George and its islands gracefully add to the picture. Boats in all sizes skim the waters--who could ask for a better place to spend a few leisure hours?

The downstairs Pub Room offers lighter suppers, sandwiches and burgers with the same attention and creativeness used in the upstairs cooking. On the walls, pictures depict the story of the updating process of the restaurant.

The architecture of the Algonquin marries the old with the new. Two separate levels of dining allows each diner a spectacular view of Lake George. The restaurant "invites" guests to stay the evening or to stop for a drink. Formal or casual, the restaurant's dining rooms meet the needs of the guests.

For two generations the Smith family restaurant had a tradition for outstanding food and service...certainly a standard worth maintaining...and definitely worth your visit.

How to get there: From Lake George Village, take Route 9 for about 9 miles to Bolton Landing. It is on the right hand side. You can't miss it! Open Thursday-Sunday during the Winter. Seven days during the Summer. Lunch. Dinner. (518) 644-9442.

While you're there: Lake George is a busy, well-known resort town. Camping. Boating. Swimming-public beach. Golf. Tennis. Attractions. Opera. Boat rides. Hot air ballooning. Snowmobiling. Ice Fishing. Cross-country skiing. Winter Carnival.

LEMON PARMESAN DRESSING

1 qt. prepared Paris dressing (vinaigrette)
2 eggs
4 lemon halves, grated
Juice of 6 lemons
2 c. olive oil
1 c. white wine vinegar
1/2 c. Parmesan cheese
2 T. basil

1. Beat ingredients together.

NOTE: It is better with fresh basil.

Makes about 2 quarts.

NOTES

DELICIOUS BUTTER ROLLS

2 eggs
3/4 c. sugar
1 t. salt, heaping
1 c. milk
1/4 lb. butter
1 large spoonful Crisco
2 cakes yeast
1/3 c. water
4 c. flour

1. Scald the milk, melt the shortening in the milk. Cool.
2. Add to beaten egg mixture.
3. Dissolve 2 cakes of yeast in 1/3 c. water.
4. Sprinkle with sugar.
5. Add 2 c. flour to egg mixture. Beat well.
6. Add yeast and 2 more c. flour. Mix well.
7. Place in refrigerator overnight.
8. Next day make rolls into any shape and let double in bulk.
9. Bake at 350° or until brown.
10. Brush with butter.

NOTE: They freeze beautifully!

Serves: 30
Preparation: 20 minutes
Cooking: 15 minutes

PLUM SAUCE

No. 10 whole pitted purple plums
1 quart orange juice
1 c. soy sauce
2 c. red wine vinegar
4 T. garlic powder
17 T. cornstarch
1 lb. brown sugar

1. Mix plums, juices, soy sauce and wine vinegar in a double boiler. Bring to boil.
2. Separately mix garlic powder, cornstarch and brown sugar.
3. Add the two mixtures in double boiler until sauce thickens.

NOTE: Use with deep fried shrimp, chicken strips or duck. Refrigeration will keep leftover for future use.

Makes 1-1/2 gallon

ZUCCHINI FROMAGE

1-1/2 lb. Swiss cheese
1/2 lb. butter
4 lbs. zucchini
Salt and pepper to taste
Bread crumbs, seasoned or unseasoned

1. Cut zucchini into strips 3"x4". Layer in bottom of ungreased casserole.
2. Salt and pepper layer.
3. Layer the grated cheese sparingly.
4. Top with bread crumbs.
5. Repeat the layers.
6. Cover with thin layer of cold butter.
7. Bake for 1 hour and 15 minutes at 350°.

NOTE: The secret is not to overcook. It should be soft but crunchy.

Serves: 6
Preparation: 25 minutes
Cooking: 1 hour 15 minutes

Established 1891

THE BALSAM HOUSE

CHESTERTOWN

In the past few years, more and more businesses in the Adirondacks--restaurants, lodges, galleries and gift shops have been staying open year round. People have been discovering the wintry side of the Adirondack area, enjoying its rural charm and participating in the Winter sports such as downhill and cross-country skiing, snowmobiling, ice fishing and skating. But, they also come for the warmth they find in the country inn known as The Balsam House, offering the comforts of "a home away from home" yet, with the scrumptious cuisine and "pampering" of a truly relaxing vacation.

The Balsam House is situated near the headwaters of the Hudson River in Chestertown, New York. It is serenely set on the private waters of Friends Lake, where visitors can partake in some of the finest smallmouth bass fishing in the State. It was originally built as a farmhouse by the Valentine family in 1845. Additions and alterations were made in 1891. It was then opened as the "Valentine Hotel", a summer resort. In 1945 the property changed owners and was renamed "Balsam House." It was operated as a Summer hotel for twenty eight years. It remained vacant for eight years then in 1980 it was purchased by Frank Ellis, the present owner.

Frank, with a designer's eye and fine taste, and the help of local artisans, completely gutted, faithfully restored and reopened as an elegant year round country inn with a new life. Retaining the character and warmth of the Victorian era, Mr. Ellis defines it as "casual elegance."

The Inn elegantly serves fine French country cuisine. As the evening approaches, the aroma from the delicacies of the kitchen will stimulate

157

your desire to experience the talents of their award winning Swiss chef, Gert Alper, hailed by several critics as a "culinary genius." The fare includes appetizers such as Pate Maison, Vol au Vent a La Reine and Coulibiac Sauce Verte. Popular entrees include Adirondack Trout, Duckling Chambertin, Sauteed Veal Kidneys, Rack of Lamb and an assortment of steaks and veal dishes. The rack of lamb has been described by one internationally known writer as "the best I've had on four continents." Another important ingredient of the Balsam House dining is the enthusiastic staff waiting to serve you. Your enjoyment is their satisfaction.

The superb quality of the food assures the restaurant's success as does the fine blending of the soft peach and navy colors and the marble fireplace in the dining room.

During this special dining evening, a light jazz piano player entertains in the cozy bar. This spirited bar, with its large stone fireplace overlooking Gore Mountain, is the icing on the evening's cake.

It is not often that you discover a place that surpasses your expectations. From the minute you arrive at The Balsam House you become totally absorbed in the atmosphere and pleasurable surroundings. The Inn seems to welcome you in the celebration of the Adirondacks. Stay the weekend, share a superb meal or just stop to enjoy a drink. It is definitely, without any doubt, an inn with an elegant flair combined with a genuine "at home" personality.

How to get there: *Take Chestertown Exit 25 off I-87. Go 4 miles West to Friends Lake. Turn left, go about 4 more miles Inn. Open year round. Lodging. Lunch. Dinner. Lounge. (518) 494-2828 or 494-4431.*

While you're there: *Sledding. Horse drawn sleigh rides. Cross-country skiing. Snowshoeing. Gore Mountain is 20 minutes drive. Summer guests enjoy carriage rides. Champagne cruises. Hot air ballooning. Horseback riding. Fishing. For those hardy people looking for a days outing nearby is Moose Pond. Here the fishing for 17 inch lake and brook trout is at the very best. It is located off the Newcomb exit. The trailhead is on the westside of Newcomb and is well marked (highway 28). This favorite stocked lake is six miles up a dirt road and can be reached by bicycle or foot only. This trail is also terrific for cross-country skiing. The Red Truck Clay Works is only three miles from the Balsam House and well worth a visit. The pottery is handmade, woodfired, functional and decorative stoneware including plenty of beautiful pieces for the home and gifts. They have demonstrations of throwing and firing when possible.*

BALSAM HOUSE ROAST DUCK CHAMBERTIN

1 - 3-1/2 to 4 pound duck
1 bottle good red cooking wine (750 ml.)
2 c. white stock or chicken bouillon stock
1/4 c. carrots, finely chopped
1/4 c. scallions, finely chopped
1/4 c. celery, finely chopped
1/2 c. seeded tomatoes, diced
Cornstarch
1 pat butter
Truffles (European mushrooms, optional)

1. Rub the duck inside and out with salt and pepper, reserving the giblets and discarding the liver.
2. Prick the duck in the sides and breast with fork to allow fat to drain while cooking.
3. Place in roasting pan and roast at 450° for one and one-half hours.
4. Remove the duck from the oven and allow it to cool off a little. Cut lengthwise in half and remove as many bones as possible.
5. Chop bones into several pieces and saute with giblets in same roasting pan, using one tablespoon of drippings from the duck. (NOTE: If the roasting pan contains burned sediment, use another pan to saute in).
6. Add three-quarters bottle of red cooking wine and white stock of chicken bouillon stock and simmer one hour, or reduced by one-half.
7. Strain stock from the pan and saute carrots, celery, scallions and tomatoes in a pat of butter.
8. Pour strained sauce over them and cook 15 minutes.
9. Thicken sauce with a little cornstarch and mix last quarter of bottle of red wine.
10. Season with salt and pepper and, if possible, add chopped truffles.

continued on next page

11. Reheat duck in very hot oven (450° to 500°) less than 5 minutes, just until the skin gets crisp.

12. Pour sauce onto plate, and put duck on top of sauce. (do not pour sauce over the duck, because it will get soggy.)

NOTE: Good luck to those of you who want to give it a shot! Remember, if it doesn't work out, there's a quaint little country inn up in the Adirondacks which serves it perfectly every time.

Serves: 2
Preparation: 1 hour
Cooking: 1-1/2 hours/1 hour and 35 minutes

GARNET HILL LODGE

NORTH RIVER

"All summer long the lakes
and woods of the region give
the solace which only nature
can give to her eager disciples.
Every vacationist has his favorite
spot and time of year. My own
is a Log House looking far
down on the gleam of Thirteenth
Lake. Set me on its porch early
on a July morning when the mists
that lie close above the surface
are breaking- and you will find
a happy man."

Pg. 215, MY KIND OF COUNTRY
By Carl Carmer, New York State
author and naturalist
David McKay & Co., publisher

Located high on a mountain top in the Southern Adirondacks, Garnet Hill Lodge affords the visitor views only a backpacking hiker usually sees after a day's climb. Now a resort center, Garnet Hill has a long history as a mining area. Garnet Hill takes its name from "Ruby of the Adirondacks"-the Garnet. This semi-precious stone, a mined product and mainstay of the area's economy for over 100 years, is found at elevations of 2400 feet. The red garnet of this area takes its color and hardness from the iron ore present. When visiting Hooper Mine, an open pit mine, or while viewing the wall from Thriteenth Lake, you will notice the reddish color of the ore from a distance. On closer observation, you will notice the deeper red pockets of garnet.

Garnets were first mined in 1879 on Gore Mountain. In September of 1893, Frank Hooper developed a mechanical liquid separation process that would efficiently recover the garnet from ore. In 1894, he established the North River Mining Company at Ruby Mountain, and, in 1905, moved the operation to the Hooper Mine at Garnet Hill. The Garnet Hill facility consisted of 55 buildings including a store, school, blacksmith shop and a three-storied boarding house. After the mine closed in 1928, the area was established as a resort community using the former miner's quarters as summer cottages. In 1936, the "Log House" was built to provide guests lodging and restaurant facilities. Today, the Garnet Hill Lodge is as busy year round as ever. There are miles and miles of hiking and cross-country ski trails. Visit their private beach-so private there are no homes or cottages along the state owned shoreline! Boats, too, are available.

George and Mary Heim, the fourth owners, have been busy there since 1977. Their warm welcome and sincere hospitality create a special appeal to the lover of the outdoors. Mary enjoys spending her hours in the kitchen. Each day she features a Log House Special, which may be anything from a tender Lamb Roast to a tangy New Orleans veal dish. Also, on the menu, is a fish of the day, delicately seasoned and poached in a special wine sauce. Homestyle favorites: spaghetti and meatballs, pork and lamb chops, and New York sirloin strip steak in two sizes.

Every Saturday night at the Log House, their famous smorgasbord is featured. The dishes vary with the seasons, but you can expect to taste the finest prepared vegetables which compliment meat and fish dishes. A salad bar, a delicious assortment of freshly baked breads and desserts offer you a memorable evening of excellent Adirondack dining. There is no doubt that the Heims deserve a standing ovation for providing such tantalizing food served in a pleasant and relaxing atmosphere amid spectacular mountain scenery.

If you are looking for just one true Adirondack experience, including wildflowers and wilderness, Garnet Hill Lodge is a precious gem.

How to get there: *From western New York, take Rt. 8 to Wevertown. From Plattsburgh and Montreal, go south on I-87 to Exit 25. Take Rt. 8 to Wevertown. From N.Y.C. take thruway north to 2nd Albany Exit 24, then north on I-87 toward Montreal to Warrensburg, Exit 23. Go north on Rt. 9 for 4-1/2 miles, then northwest on Rt. 28 to Wevertown. Continue on Rt. 28 to North River, go past the post office and turn left on the 13th Lake Road. Follow to top of hill. Rooms. Cottages. The restaurant serves three meals to travelers and guests. Full service bar. Cross-country skihaus. (518) 251-2821.*

While you're there: *Hiking. Fishing. White water rafting and tubing. Swimming. Boating. Canoeing. Sailing. Tennis. Skiing at Gore Mountain. Cross-country ski rentals. Trails. Tours of Barton's Garnet Mine.*

SAUTEED LEEKS

2 lb. fresh leeks
2 large onions, chopped
1/2 c. olive oil
3 medium carrots, sliced
1 large tomato or No. 2 can whole tomatoes
1 t. salt
1/4 t. white pepper

1. Wash leeks thoroughly. Discard green top. Cut white and light green parts into 2" pieces. Soak in cold water.
2. Saute chopped onion in olive oil for 15 minutes.
3. Add carrots, tomato, drained leeks, salt, and pepper. Cover vegetables with boiling water. Cover pan tightly.
4. Steam vegetables for 1 to 1-1/2 hours.

NOTE: Maybe served over hot rice. Excellent with broiled fish.

Serves: 6
Preparation: 15 minutes
Cooking: 15 minutes/1 - 1-1/2 hours

TEA ROOM CARROT BREAD

2 c. flour
1-1/2 c. sugar
2 t. soda
2 t. cinnamon
1/2 t. salt
2 c. carrots, finely grated
1/4 c. nuts, chopped (optional)
1/2 c. coconut, shredded
1/2 c. raisins, (optional)
1 c. cooking oil
1 t. vanilla
3 eggs, slightly beaten

1. Sift flour, sugar, soda, cinnamon, and salt together in large bowl.
2. Stir in carrots. Add nuts, coconut, and raisins.
3. Pour into greased 9x5x3 loaf pan.
4. Bake at 350° for 1 hour.

Serves: 12-14
Preparation: 20 minutes
Cooking: 1 hour

ORANGE RYE BREAD

2-3/4 c. warm water
2 pkgs. dry yeast
1/2 c. firmly packed brown sugar
3 T. soft margarine
4 t. salt
3 T. orange peel, grated
1/3 c. dark molasses
3-3/4 c. rye flour, unsifted
5-1/2 to 6-1/2 c. white flour, unsifted

1. Measure warm water into large bowl. Sprinkle in yeast.
2. Stir until dissolved. Stir in sugar, salt, margarine, orange peel, molasses, and rye flour.
3. Beat until blended. Stir in white flour to make stiff dough.
4. Turn onto floured board and knead until smooth and elastic about 10 to 12 minutes.
5. Place in greased bowl. Cover and let rise until double in bulk - about 1 hour.
6. Punch down and divide in half.
7. Roll each half to a 14x9 inch rectangle.
8. Shape into loaves - 9x5x3 inch.
9. Cover and let rise in warm place about 1 hour and 10 minutes.
10. Bake on lowest rack at 375° about 40 minutes.

Makes: 2 loaves
Preparation: 40 minutes
Cooking: 40 minutes

THE GEORGIAN

LAKE GEORGE

Lake George, a miniature resort town in Warren County is known for two reasons. One is for the scenic beauty of Lake George which attracts an ever increasing Summer population. And the other is The Georgian Restaurant located in the Village directly on the lake.

A perennial award winner and favorite of residents and out-of-towners, The Georgian, has carefully combined exquisite dining and nightly stageshow entertainment to make an evening out truly a celebration.

The restaurant's decor is echoed with tablecloths and napkins in two blues, owner designed Jackson china in formal blue and gold complimented by fine crystal goblets and enhanced by the uses of pewter.

The cuisine at the Georgian is Europen influenced French and American recipes. Karl Rosin has been the head chef for twenty three years. Karl is the recipient of many national and international awards. Among them is the 1983 Escoffier Award, that being, the second highest international award. Other distinguished awards for his excellence is the Silver Spoon award which he received for three consecutive years. He has been the chef of the year and holds the position of certified executive chef.

Offering over thirty-five entrees, such as Veal Scallopine a la Georgian which is tender slices of veal sauteed with mushrooms and shallots, seasoned in heavy cream and sherry wine served on broccoli spears, or Lobster Cantonese, a whole fresh Maine lobster in a tempting oriental lobster sauce served on a bed of steamed rice, one no longer wonders why this delightful restaurant receives award after award including

AAA's Four Diamond Award year after year.

The Georgian and its formal touch is the work of Orvil Penrose, owner and president, who is kept busy with the restaurant as well as managing the adjoining motel. I met with Orvil, a savvy man who one might expect to be more at home in the city than involved in hotel and restaurant operations in this small community.

To dine at the Georgian in its fashionable formality, in a setting overlooking beautiful Lake George is an evening's celebration at its best we all well deserve...cocktails...a gourmet dinner...a stage show...dancing ...and we all do deserve the best!

How to get there: Go to Lake George Village. 384 Canada St. Open May-October. Gourmet Dining. Dancing. Entertainment. Lounge. Swimming Pool overlooking Lake George. Motel. (518) 668-5401.

While you're there: Boating. Fishing. Swimming. Horseback Riding. Theater. Alpine and Cross-country skiing. Snowmobiling. Ice Fishing. Hiking Trails. Attractions.

VEAL ESCALLOPINI A LA GEORGIAN

1-1/2 lbs. veal
3 T. butter, melted
12 shallots, sliced thin (fine)
12 medium mushrooms, sliced
1 T. flour
3 c. light cream (or half and half)
2 oz. dry sherry wine
Salt and white pepper

1. Brown shallots and mushrooms with butter until light brown.
2. Add flour and simmer 5 minutes.
3. Add cream, simmer 5 more minutes and add sherry wine.
4. Flatten veal slices down that have been dipped in flour.
5. In separate pan add butter and brown.
6. Cook the veal in the sauce for 5 minutes. When sauce gets too thick, add 1/2 c. more cream.

NOTE: Serve with broccoli spears.

Serves: 4
Preparation: 20 minutes
Cooking: 15 minutes

BEEF STROGANOFF

SAUCE
2 T. butter, melted
1 T. flour
1 medium onion, chopped fine
2 c. beef stock
1 T. mustard (Mister Mustard)
2 T. heavy sour cream
Salt and black pepper

1. Brown together the onion and butter until light brown.
2. Add the flour and cook 5 minutes until mixture begins to thicken.
3. Add 2 c. beef stock with 2 tablespoons of sour cream. Simmer very gently without boiling.

MEAT
1 lb. tenderloin strips, cut 2"x1/2"
2 T. butter

1. In pan with butter lightly brown.
2. Mix together with sauce and cook very slow for 2 minutes. Do not boil.

NOTE: Goes very nicely with buttered noodles or rice pilaf.

Serves: 4
Preparation: 20 minutes

IRONDEQUOIT CLUB INN

PISECO LAKE

The Irondequoit Club Inn, thirteen miles, southeast of Speculator, is indeed a truly unpretentious lodge house. Piseco, located in the heart of the southern Adirondacks, is a small community with no more than three hundred year round residents. Though the number of vacationers swells in the Summer, the Irondequoit Club Inn and the surrounding area remains one of the most unspoiled, wild, remote sections of the Adirondack Forest Preserve.

The Club, an 1800 farmhouse, was established in 1892 by a group of New York City men who enjoyed the outdoor life. Today, it is owned by the Piseco Corporation whose members continue to enjoy this unspoiled six hundred acre resort on Piseco Lake.

Pulling up a rocking chair on the wide sunny porch offers you an unexcelled view of the lake and surrounding mountain forest. While experiencing the view of this serene, unspoiled wilderness lake listen to some of the older guests relate their reminiscence of the "old days" they enjoyed here as children-the "stuff memories are made of."

As you enter, you'll be greeted warmly by Diane Clauson who graciously leads you into the living room. A large fireplace, high ceilings, antiques, Adirondack pictures and momentos-along with the dining atmosphere- give the Irondequoit a boarding house feeling which you might have experienced out of your past. If you came from a large family you'll know and understand.

Entering the large fireplaced dining room, you may be seated at one of the large tables. If you don't like eating with strangers, you should bring a group of friends, but, then you'll miss a part of the eating fun at this friendly family style inn.

Diane and Andy do all the cooking together. Diane loves the baking, and from talking with her, I would say it was a "labor of love." Roasted meats and freshly cooked vegetables along with garden salads, hot homemade rolls, muffins and scrumptious desserts.

On Sundays, during the Summer at 6:00 P.M. a delicious barbeque is served outside. After a game or two of tennis on the private courts or a swim in the sandy beach lake, what could be more inviting than a multitude of good food and new friendships?

If you like large family style Thanksgiving dinners, you'll love the warm sharing atmosphere at the Irondequoit Inn.

Stay for a meal, overnight or a week-there is plenty of room and a mass of outdoor activities in the "down home" remote Adirondack Inn. If a homelike atmosphere, friendly faces and an abundance of delicious food is to your liking, the Irondequoit wants you.

How to get there: *From Hwy. 8 follow signs to Piseco Lake. the Irondequoit is just past the small village. Breakfast. Lunch. Dinner. Rooms. Cottages. Efficiencies. Tent Sites. Sandy Beach. Dock. Tennis Courts. Horseshoes. Recreation Room. Open July 1st to Labor Day. Weekends and for special groups. Winter Ski Weekends. Call first. (518) 548-5500.*

While you're there: *Not far away is a club owned island for exploring and picnicking. Fifteen minutes to a sporty nine hole golf course. Fish in Piseco Lake include Lake and Rainbow trout, small mouthed bass, pike, pickerel, whitefish, bullhead and sunfish. Canoeing. Boating. Hiking trails.*

QUICK ROLLS

1-1/2 c. flour
1 t. salt
2 T. yeast
2 T. sugar
1-1/2 c. water
1-1/2 T. oil
1 beaten whole egg

1. Mix together flour, salt, yeast and sugar.
2. Add water (100 degrees) and mix well.
3. Add oil and mix well.
4. Add flour and mix well.
5. Knead for 5 minutes and add more flour if necessary.
6. Let double in bulk in a warm place. Then punch down.
7. Pinch off 1" diameter balls of dough and place on greased baking pan, just touching each other.
8. Let rise again to approximately double. Brush with beaten egg.
9. Bake in hot oven 425° until brown.

Serves: 12
Preparation: 15 minutes
Cooking: 12-15 minutes

PORK CHOP CASSEROLE

8 pork chops
16 baby potatoes, parboiled
2 lbs. of spinach, fresh
3 c. cream sauce*
2 T. cheddar cheese

1. Braise the chops.
2. Remove chops from pan and brown the potatoes.
3. Blanch the fresh spinach.
4. In large baking dish, place spinach, then potatoes with chops on top.
5. Cover with cream sauce, sprinkle with cheese and bake at 375° for 50 minutes.

*See glossary

Serves: 4
Preparation: 30 minutes
Cooking: 50 minutes

APPLE WALNUT PIE

5 apples
1/4 c. orange juice
1 t. cinnamon
1/4 t. nutmeg
1/4 t. ground cloves
1/4 c. butter
1 c. brown sugar
3 eggs
1/2 c. light corn syrup
1-1/2 c. walnuts
1/2 t. salt
1 t. vanilla

1. Prepare a 10 inch pie shell.
2. Prepare the bottom layer of the pie: pare and slice thin about 5 apples.
3. In the orange juice mix the brown sugar, cinnamon, nutmeg and ground cloves, stir into apples and put in bottom of pie shell.
4. Prepare the top layer: In a mixing bowl, cream butter and sugar. Continue beating and add eggs, corn syrup, walnuts, salt and vanilla.
5. Pour over apple mixture.
6. Bake at 375° for 50-60 minutes or until golden brown and inserted knife comes out clean.

Serves: 6
Preparation: 30 minutes
Cooking: 50-60 minutes

MELODY LODGE

Hamilton County is the second largest county in the Adirondacks with the lowest population. Located in this forested and rocky Southern Adirondack county is the pond-pocked Village of Speculator. The population is about 350 year round residents, but during the warmer months vacationers, campers and tourists swarm into this inviting primitive area by the thousands to fish the lakes, to climb the many mountain trails and to camp at Moffit's State Park. Many stay all summer long in the private cottages that dot the shores of the Sacandaga Lake. (Do not confuse this Sacandaga Lake with the Greater Sacandaga Lake, this is the original.)

In 1924, Gene Tunney, the famous heavyweight boxing champion was just one person who spent time training in Speculator. Soon, many other boxers came to Speculator to train, bringing fame to this small resort town.

Set high upon Page Mountain, just North of Speculator (on Route 30), Melody Lodge overlooks both the Sacandaga Lake and Lake Pleasant. It was built in 1912 as a singing school for girls. During the Summer months, the mountainside echoed with voices of young hopefuls.

Today, one of the pleasures, as you tour this beautiful, serene lake area is to enjoy a memorable dining evening at Melody Lodge. A spacious restaurant lodge with spectacular lake views offer the diner a popular menu, unbeatable salads, homemade hot breads and heavenly desserts all at reasonable prices.

Eight years ago, George and Sue Swift and their growing family moved from Westport, Connecticut to Speculator's Melody Lodge. All the cooking is done by George and his chef-helper, Tom Higgins. Their combined culinary wizardry features a variety of entree choices including broiled lamb chops, chicken, baked ham and roast beef. Fresh seafood is in abundance from Bay Scallops to George's famous Scampi prepared from his own recipe. You could travel all over the Adirondacks and never find the same delicious recipe he has perfected. One of Tom's inspirational specialties is the "Mexican Fiesta Evening" complete with an entire menu of Mexican drinks, appetizers and entrees. It has become a very popular evening and is now a regular feature.

Sue does all the baking...breads, rolls, desserts. Lemon Meringue, Apple, Blueberry and Creme de Menthe pies are some of her delicious favorites.

Melody Lodge is a restaurant lavish in food, but simple in decor. Antiques, rustic pine paneling and large stone fireplaces create a warmth and style of country casualness. This, combined with the touch of excellent chefs and staff serving savory meals, is the perfect choice for a special dining experience in Speculator. From the moment of arrival, Melody Lodge creates a worthy dining experience to delight every appetite, as well as, the tastebuds. Speculator provides the chance for you to relate to nature and its beauty in your own fashion.

How to get there: *Routes 28 and 30 meet at the crossroads in the center of Speculator. Drive 1 mile North on Route 30. Watch for sign. Rooms. Lunch. Dinner. Cocktail Lounge. Open 7 days a week in the Summer. Closed Tues. and Wed. during the Winter. (518) 548-6562.*

While you're there: *Camping at Mofitt's State Campground. White water rafting. Fishing. Boating. Hiking. Bicycling. A "Fly In" seminar for seaplanes is held at the end of June. Rides offered. 4th of July parade. In February, there are snowmobile races. Oak Mountain Ski Hill. Many cross-country trails.*

EGGPLANT CASSEROLE

1 medium eggplant, peeled and cubed
1-15 oz. can of stewed tomatoes
1 green pepper, seeded, and sliced
8 oz. sharp New York State cheddar cheese, grated
1 medium onion, sliced
2-3 slices of white bread

1. Cook eggplant in boiling salted water until tender. Drain well.
2. Pour stewed tomatoes in 2 qt. casserole.
3. Break up bread into casserole so juice is absorbed.
4. Stir fry green pepper in hot oil in frying pan until tender-crisp.
5. Add green pepper, onion mixture, and eggplant to stewed tomatoes and bread in casserole.
6. Add cheddar cheese. Stir to mix well.
7. Bake at 350° until bubbly and hot (about 1/2 hour).

Serves: 6
Preparation: 25 minutes
Cooking: 30 minutes

EMMANUEL LABOR'S
MEXICAN PIZZA

4-10" flour tortillas
1-1/2 lbs. ground beef
1 c. refried beans
1/2 c. diced onions
1 c. green chillies, diced
2 tomatoes, diced
1 bunch scallions, chopped fine
1 T. garlic powder
1 t. crushed red pepper
1 t. oregano
2 jalapeno peppers, finely chopped (optional)
Salt and pepper to taste
1/2 c. tomato juice
2 lbs. shredded yellow cheese
1 lb. Monterey Jack cheese

1. Preheat oven to 350°.
2. Deep fry tortillas to a golden brown on both sides. Drain and set aside.
3. Combine ground beef, beans, onions, 1/2 c. green chiles, garlic powder, red pepper, jalapenos, salt and pepper and oregano in large frying pan. Cook over medium heat until browned, using potato masher to separate beef. Pour off grease.
4. Add tomato juice and beans. Mix thoroughly while heating.
5. Place mixture evenly on flour tortillas. Cover with cheddar cheese, then add Monterey Jack, remaining chiles, tomatoes and scallions.
6. Bake in 350° oven for 7 minutes or until cheeses are melted.
7. Quarter each pizza. Serve with sour cream and salsa.

Serves: 6
Preparation: 45 minutes
Cooking: 7 minutes

HOMEMADE APPLE PIE

6-8 firm apples depending on size (Northern Spies are good)
1-1/2 c. sugar
1 t. cinnamon
2 T. flour
2 T. butter
1 T. sugar
Your favorite pie crust.

1. Mix cut up apples with sugar (depending on taste), cinnamon and flour.
2. Fill pie shell with mixture, dot with butter, top with upper crust, seal edges with fork, prick top crust with fork so steam can escape.
3. Brush with milk and sprinkle 1 tablespoon of sugar on top.
4. Bake in a very hot oven about 425 for 15 minutes and reduce heat to 325° for about 45 minutes or until apples are tender. Cool before cutting.

NOTE: Pie may be warmed after cooling. This prevents the juices from running out.

Serves: 8
Preparation: 25 minutes
Cooking: 15 minutes at 425°/45 minutes at 325°

MAPLE WALNUT CHIFFON PIE

3 eggs, separated
1 c. light brown sugar, divided
1 pkg. gelatin, unflavored
1/4 c. water
Pinch of salt
1-1/4 t. maple flavoring
1 c. heavy cream, whipped
1/4-1/2 c. walnuts, finely chopped
8 walnut halves
1 baked 9" pie shell
Additional whipped cream for garnish

1. In top part of double boiler, mix salt, 1/2 c. brown sugar and gelatin.
2. Add water, egg yolks, slightly beaten.
3. Stir over simmering water about 5 minutes or until gelatin is dissolved and mixture is slightly thickened. Remove from heat.
4. Add maple flavoring and cool.
5. Beat egg whites with 1/2 c. brown sugar till stiff.
6. Fold together gelatin mixture, whipped cream, chopped nuts and beaten egg whites.
7. Pour into pie shell and chill several hours.
8. Garnish with dabs of whipped cream and walnut halves for each serving.

Serves: 8
Preparation: 30 minutes
Cooking: 5 minutes

MERRILL MAGEE HOUSE

WARRENSBURG

In New York's southern Adirondacks is the peaceful village of Warrensburg. It is known for three things. First, it is the antique center of the Adirondacks with many individual shops and their specialties, within walking distance of each other offering terrific bargains to those "antique hounds" and browsers. From American folk art, prints and books to estate jewelry, toys, tools and dolls the ancient "ready to buy collections" give an extra joy to vacationers. Secondly, Warrensburg sponsors the "World's Largest Garage Sale" the first week in October. With over 400 exhibits the two day street sale and auction brings tourists and antiquers from a half dozen states.

In the center of town next to the bandstand another pleasing adventure of an earlier era awaits those who open the gate and step behind the white picket fence.

The Merrill Magee House, a beautiful 19th century house in a park like setting is much the same today. The house abounds with lovely antiques, original wallpaper and glowing fireplaces offering the charm of a different dining experience.

You may want to enjoy your meal on the screened porch overlooking the park, the bandstand and pool. Historically, in 1900, the Merrill family was so fond of this room, once used as a summer kitchen, they had it moved from Thurman Station five miles away. The room dates back to 1873.

Inside, the English dining room candlelit tables dressed in pink and rose linens offer a country charm to match the tastefully prepared meals.

The innkeepers, Florence and Ken Carrington have a very talented

183

daughter, Pam who prepares the meals. You will find a touch of England on the dinner menu, such as Beef Wellington, an individual tenderloin of beef layered with goose liver pate and wrapped in a golden puff pastry or Chicken Queen Elizabeth, a tender breast of chicken filled with ham and cheese sauteed and served with a wine sauce. Pam's emphasis is on serving the highest quality fresh foods, which change daily with the season and availability at the market.

Do not pass up one of the rich "prepared in the kitchen" desserts. Brandy Walnut Pie and Strawberry Pie are among the favorites and certainly worth the calories.

After dinner, stop in the cozy pine and pewter tavern for a bit of after dinner fellowship. Relax by the cheery fire and reflect on the day's activities or stop by the kitchen and say "hello" to Pam, the "chef genius" at the Merrill Magee House.

How to get there: *Exit 23 off Interstate 87. 2 Hudson St., Warrensburg, next to the bandstand. Lunch. Dinner. Afternoon Tea. Sunday Brunch. Rooms. Lounge. Gift Shop. Open year round. (518) 623-2449.*

While you're there: *Cross-country skiing. (Skis can be rented at the Inn.) Downhill skiing at Gore Mountain, Hickory Hill and West Mountain. Hiking. Boating. Fishing. Museums. Opera. Antiquing.*

CARROT PINEAPPLE CAKE

1-1/2 c. flour
1 c. sugar
1 t. baking powder
1 t. baking soda
1 t. cinnamon
1/2 t. salt
2/3 c. cooking oil
2 eggs
1 c. carrots, finely shredded
1/2 c. pineapple juice
1 t. vanilla

1. In a large bowl stir together all dry ingredients.
2. Add eggs, oil, carrots, pineapple and vanilla.
3. Mix until moistened.
4. Beat with electric mixer 2 minutes at medium speed.
5. Pour into 9"x9"x2" pan or bundt pan and bake at 350° for 35 minutes.

CREAM CHEESE FROSTING

3 oz. cream cheese
4 T. butter
1 t. vanilla
Dash of salt
2-1/2 c. powdered sugar

1. Cream together a 3 ounce package of cream cheese softened and 4 tablespoons soft butter or margarine.
2. Beat in vanilla and dash of salt.
3. Gradually add powdered sugar and blend well.

Serves: 9
Preparation: 15 minutes
Cooking: 35 minutes

BRANDY PECAN PIE

3 eggs
1 c. sugar
1/2 t. salt
2 T. butter, melted
1/2 c. dark corn syrup
1/2 c. whipping cream
1 t. vanilla
1/2 c. brandy
1 c. pecan halves, chopped

1. Beat eggs, sugar, salt, butter, syrup and cream.
2. Stir in vanilla, brandy and pecans.
3. Pour into uncooked pastry pie shell.
4. Bake 40-50 minutes at 375°.

NOTE: Filling should be set and the crust should be brown.

Serves: 6
Preparation: 12 minutes
Cooking: 40-50 minutes

NOTES

BANANA NUT BREAD

1-1/2 c. butter
2 c. sugar
8 eggs, beaten
2 t. salt
2 t. baking soda
3-1/2 t. baking powder
6 c. flour
4 c. bananas, mashed
1-1/2 c. nuts, chopped

1. Beat butter and sugar together.
2. Add eggs to butter and sugar mixture and set aside.
3. Mix all dry ingredients together.
4. Add dry mixture gradually to the butter mixture.
5. Add bananas and nuts to mixture.
6. Bake at 350° for 45 minutes in a greased and floured pan.

Serves: Makes 3 loaves
Preparation: 15 minutes
Cooking: 45 minutes

NOTES

OLDE SCHOOLHOUSE
RESTAURANT

Less than two generations ago, many New York children began their formal education in a one-room schoolhouse. Of all our public buildings, not one holds more memories as readily, for so many people, than the one room building with one teacher educating all the children in all subjects of learning. Memories of a more carefree childhood begin here-one's first venture away from the family.

Street Road School, located halfway between Crown Point and Ticonderoga, is such a school, originally built in 1882, it was a two room schoolhouse. After the "baby boom" of World War II, an addition was built.

Eventually time changed this earlier concept of education. The buildings, once occupied by the children (socializing and learning) were abandoned for new concepts in educations. But today, the Olde Schoolhouse is alive again with happy sounds and pleasing aromas! It offers you a walk back into yesteryear. Generous portions of homecooked food are served to you by genial hosts, Bob and Milly Hill. All of the dishes including: roast beef, steak and poultry entrees, are prepared in the Schoolhouse kitchen by Bob himself. You won't find anything tastier than Milly's generous open steak sandwich or today's lighter favorite of thick soup and fresh salad. For dessert, feast on the oversized apple dumpling made of flaky light pastry crust, crowned with a red sauce and mounds of whipped cream! Their specialties are unique.

Prepared with the freshest ingredients, they are priced to make them very "special" for the excellent quality.

Dress is as casual as the atmosphere. The service and food are everything. The Olde Schoolhouse Restaurant is not for the thin-skinned gourmet, but, for the connoisseur of delectable meals with that special American "down home flavorsome taste."

How to get there: *On Rt. 9 and Rt. 22, north of Ticonderoga. Street Road. Lounge. Lunches. Dinners. Open year round. (518) 585-4044.*

While you're there: *Fort Ticonderoga is a restored fortress and national landmark. It illustrates the founding of this nation from the Colonial Wars through the American Revolution. Located on a hill overlooking Lake Champlain the fort should be a "must day trip" as a walk back in American history. On Lake Champlain. Boating. Fishing. Swimming. Camping. Golf. Theater. Festivals.*

CHICKEN PARMIGAN

2 chicken breasts, split and deboned
2 eggs, whipped
1/2 c. bread crumbs
1/2 c. flour
1 T. garlic powder
1/2 t. paprika
1 t. pepper
1 t. salt
4 slices mozzarella cheese
2 c. spaghetti sauce (homemade or canned)

1. Combine bread crumbs, flour and all seasonings together on large plate. Dip chicken breast into whipped eggs and then into coating mix.
2. Bake at 350° for 30 minutes until done.
3. Place on plate and cover each breast with one slice of cheese and then with one-half cup of sauce.
4. Return to oven until cheese melts.

Serves: 4
Preparation: 12 minutes
Cooking: 30 minutes

SPLIT PEA SOUP

1 c. split peas
2-4 c. water
3 c. milk or non dairy creamer
1 carrot
1 small onion, cut up
1 ham bone
Salt and pepper to taste
1/2 t. celery salt

1. Wash peas a few times with cold water and place them in a large kettle with water and soak overnight.
2. The following day, add carrot, onion and ham bone.
3. Cook over medium heat until it boils, then let simmer until the peas are tender. About 1-3/4 hours uncovered.
4. Remove ham bone and pick meat from bone. Press everything through a sieve and return everything to the pot.
5. Add seasonings, milk and meat.
6. Stir until thickened.

Serves: 6
Preparation: Soak over night/10 minutes
Cooking: 3 hours

NAVY BEAN SOUP

1 lb. dried navy beans
5 c. water
1 can beef consomme
4 potatoes, diced
2 onions, diced
1/4 c. butter
4 carrots
2 c. ham from ham bone, cut up
2 bay leaves
Salt and pepper to taste

1. Place beans in water and simmer for two hours.
2. First add potatoes to soup. Then, saute onions until partially cooked and add to soup with all other ingredients.
3. Simmer another hour until all the vegetables are done.

Serves: 6
Preparation: 10 minutes
Cooking: 3 hours

SKENE MANOR

WHITEHALL

Skene Manor has wonderful food, a cozy bar, a mountain top setting and an antique filled dining room with a cheery fireplace. With all that you might wonder what else can be said. Plenty!

Joel and Peggy Murphy are newcomers to the Adirondacks, having recently decided to shift from the faster pace urban life of New Jersey for the simple rural life of Whitehall. They came with their family to learn the restaurant business. They bought the historical Skene Manor.

Anyone who has done any traveling in New York State and Washington County has driven by The Skene Manor. It is the stately mansion situated on Skene Mountain, a site of British and Colonial troop battles and Indian encampments, overlooking the small, but picturesque town of Whitehall. Skene Manor is so different from the other restaurants that you wouldn't expect to find anything like it, least of all, in rural New York State.

It was built by New York State Supreme Court Judge, Joseph Potter in 1872. Laborers were brought from Italy to construct the three story, granite building furnished with mahogany panels, floors of parquetry, tapestries and Italian marble fireplaces. It was named after the founder of Whitehall (originally Skenesborough) Colonel Philip Skene, a British Army officer of the Revolutionary War.

It was in the very shadow of Skene Mountain that Colonel Skene built the first ship to sail on Lake Champlain. This schooner was captured by Ethan Allen's troops and later became the nucleus of the FIRST AMERICAN FLEET built by Benedict Arnold in Skenesborough, the BIRTHPLACE OF THE UNITED STATES NAVY.

Skene Manor is renowned throughout the Northern New York resort area, not only, for its architectural splendor, but also, for its excellent cuisine.

Your meal will begin with sharp cheddar cheese and an assortment of crackers, soon to be followed with cups of Cream of Spinach soup and accompanied by large homemade rolls, served warm in a linen covered basket. Following a tossed salad with house made dressing, comes an apple fritter served with heated maple syrup-a superb work of art itself. Next, a relish cart is pulled to your table filled with corn relish, cottage cheese, hot peppers, applesauce and garbanzo peas.

Try the lamb chops and mint jelly for your entree. The thick chops are enormous, and the meat is tender, flavored with a variety of seasonings. It is served with a choice of potato and vegetable.

Other entree choices include Roast Western Prime Ribs of Beef au Jus (on the weekends), Chicken and Eggplant Parmigiana, Shrimp Scampi, Stuffed or Fried, or a variety of pasta selections.

The quality and quantity of superb food assures the restaurant's success. Peggy is continually experimenting with the ordinary favorites, adding her combinations and seasonings which give the food an extraordinary taste.

Another story in a number of New York State histories states that Colonel Skene kept his wife in a leaden coffin in a corner room of his garrison after her death. It is said, this was done to retain an annuity granted her as long as she should "remain above ground." According to legend, this coffin was eventually brought from the garrison located at the foot of Skene Mountain and interred in one of the cavernous recesses of the basement of Skene Manor. Here it rested for nearly one hundred years. At the time the mansion was converted into a restaurant and upon the whim of the original restauranter, the coffin was brought from the basement and placed upright in the corner of the taproom to form a base for a garnet rock waterfalls surrounding it.

Upon reflection, in what better spot could the coffin be placed? For in the taproom, the ghost of Mrs. Skene could be appeased by the mirth and fellowship of the bar. There is talk of apparations and unearthly sounds emanating from the staircase behind the waterfalls.

Whether you are seeing New York State for the first time or a long time resident looking for something out of the ordinary, a visit to Skene Manor is not to be missed. Great food at a moderate price, fresh flowers, linens and a staff that really cares...it all adds up to Skene Manor...and, in all of the Adirondacks, there's only one.

How to get there: *Drive to Whitehall by way of Rts. 4 or 22. On the Mountain. Look for signs. You can't miss it! Overlooking the canal between Lake Champlain and Lake George and Whitehall. Dinner. Lounge. (518) 499-1112.*

While you're there: *Wilson Castle Museum, restored with antiques is about 10 miles. Killington Ski Center is one-half hour. Lake George is 23 miles. Golfing next to the Manor. Camping. Excellent countryside views.*

CHICKEN FRANCAIS

1 boneless chicken breast
Flour
Egg
Bread crumbs
Butter
Mushrooms
Lemon, sliced
1/2 oz. sherry

1. Pound the chicken breast thin.
2. Dip in flour, then egg and flavored bread crumbs.
3. In frying pan, add butter and saute chicken until golden brown.
4. Top with sliced mushrooms and thinly sliced lemons.
5. Squeeze a quarter of a lemon on to chicken.
6. Add cooking sherry and simmer for 5 minutes.

Serves: 1
Preparation: 25 minutes

PECAN PIE

3 eggs
1 c. sugar
Dash of salt
1 t. vanilla
2 c. dark Karo syrup
2 T. butter, melted
1 c. pecans, broken

1. Mix all the ingredients and add pecans. Mix well.
2. Pour into unbaked 9" pie crust.
3. Bake 10 minutes at 400°, then 350° for 45 minutes.

Serves: 6-8
Preparation: 10 minutes
Cooking: 10 minutes at 400°/45 minutes at 350°

NOTES

APPLE FRITTERS

3 c. flour
3/4 c. sugar
1 t. cinnamon
3 t. baking powder
1 egg
2 apples, grated
Milk

1. Mix all the ingredients.
2. When dough is about the same as donut consistency, drop into deep fryer (300 degrees) for 3 minutes. Test with fork.
3. Serve with pure maple syrup.

Serves: 15
Preparation: 10 minutes
Cooking: 3 minutes

NOTES

Top Notch Tavern

R.J. Lamonda

TOP NOTCH TAVERN

WEST GALLWAY

A year round winner and favorite of southern Adirondackers and visitors is the Top Notch Tavern. The best elements of an earlier Americana are combined to enhance your dining pleasure. The owners, Audrey and Bob Rudolph and their son, Lynn, have created a friendly atmosphere in this one hundred year old restaurant.

There is a story of the Top Notch Tavern having a ghost. On December 7, 1885, six year old, Lucinda "Lucy" Harris died, and was buried under the Tavern. A few years ago, one of the waiters recalled a strange occurrence! It was his duty to blow out all the table candles before leaving for the night. He climbed the stairs to the upstairs dining room, blew out the candles, and returned downstairs. Being a conscientious employee, he climbed the stairs again, only to find, one of the candles still lit. He blew out the candle again and returned downstairs a second time. On a hunch, he returned upstairs a third time--the same candle was still burning! A ghost? I'll leave that up to you. Before entering the dining room, look behind the coats in the outer hall, and you will see Lucy's gravestone. If it is Lucy's ghost playing tricks, she must be glad that she has a home filled with happiness and so many good things to eat.

The Top Notch Tavern is noted for its delectable Prime Rib, but endorses eighteen other entree offerings, including a "Specialty for Two"; Prime Rib, Alaskan king crab legs, Lobster tails and Steamed Clams. It's nothing short of a Roman feast! The freshest "all you can eat" (clean your own) shrimp is just one of the luscious appetizers offered at the bread and salad bar. Saturdays and special holidays are excluded.

Lest we forget--the desserts--Top Notch homemade Hot Fudge Cake is a favorite, as well as, the traditional American homemade pies and Strawberry Shortcake.

Woodburning stoves and wall hung antiques add to the pleasure of dining in the Tavern's Americana informality. The Top Notch Tavern makes all your dining dreams come true.

How to get there: *From Saratoga Springs, take Route 29 for 17 miles to Gallway, turn left on 147 and travel 7 miles to West Gallway. Turn right at the light at the intersection in the middle of town and follow signs to the Tavern. Closed Mondays. Dinner. Lounge. (518) 842-8915.*

While you're there: *Downtown Saratoga Springs has been refurbished with a quaint shopping area. Saratoga horse racing. National Museum of Racing. Saratoga Performing Arts Center. Mineral Baths at the Saratoga State Park.*

CREAMED POTATOES

2 T. butter
2 T. flour , *CORN Starch, Arrow Root* [*1 tsp 1 tsp 1 tsp*]
3/4 c. milk
2 T. parsley
1-1/2 T. onion salt
2/3 c. mild cheese
5-6 potatoes, cooked

1. Cook potatoes.
2. Melt butter over low heat.
3. Stirring constantly and slow, add milk.
4. Add cheese and seasonings.
5. Simmer until thickened and smooth.
6. Add chopped, cooked potatoes.

NOTE: Very good using half and half instead of milk.

Serves: 4
Preparation: 10 minutes
Cooking: 35 minutes

STUFFED BAKED POTATOES

4 potatoes, baked
2 T. butter
3/4 c. half and half
2/3 c. mild cheese, grated
1-1/2 T. onion salt
Salt and pepper
A pinch of baking powder

1. Bake potatoes.
2. Cut open and remove insides.
3. Beat insides using beater.
4. Add remaining ingredients.
5. Beat well and spoon back into potato skins.

Serves: 4
Preparation: 15 minutes
Cooking: 1 hour

NOTES

NOTES

206

GLOSSARY OF TERMS

APPETIZER - A small serving of food before the entree or as the first course of a meal.

BASIC BEEF STOCK -
1-1/2 lbs. beef bones
2 carrots
1 onion
2 stalks of celery, chopped
1 garlic clove
2 tomatoes
1 bay leaf
1 t. thyme
1 t. oregano
1 t. chipped peppercorns

1. Place all ingredients in a large soup pot.
2. Add 3-4 quarts of cold water
3. Bring to boil and simmer 8-10 hours, until meat falls off the bones.
4. Strain, season with salt and pepper and use in recipes.

BEARNAISE SAUCE -
2/3 c. butter
3 egg yolks
3 t. lemon juice
Salt and pepper
1 T. tarragon vinegar
1 t. parsley
1 t. tarragon
1 t. chervil

1. In top of double boiler, melt one half of the butter. Beat in eggs and juice.
2. Add remaining butter slowly, beating constantly until mixture thickens. Do not let the water boil.
3. Stir in seasonings.
     Yield: 3/4 cup

BLANCH - To remove skins by boiling, then draining and rinsing in very cold water.

BOUILLON - Clear soup made from beef, fish or chicken.

CARAMELIZE - To melt sugar slowly over low heat until it melts and is brown in color.

CHICKEN STOCK -
1 large heavy fowl
1 onion, chopped
2 carrots, chopped
Basil
2 bay leaves
Thyme

1. Place fowl into a large soup pot.
continued on next page

2. Add onion, carrots, celery and spices.

3. Add 3 quarts of water and bring to a boil. Then simmer for 2 hours.

4. Remove fowl and strain the broth. Let stand for a few minutes and skim off chicken fat from the broth and set aside to be used for sauteing the vegetable for your soup.

5. Now you have a clear stock. This may be cooked longer to have a stronger stock.

COCKTAIL - A beverage served before dinner.

CLARIFY - To make a clear liquid by heating and removing all sediment and strain.

CREAM SAUCE -
6 T. butter
2 T. flour
1-1/2 c. thin cream

1. Melt butter and add flour and cook until it bubbles.

2. Remove from heat, slowly stirring all the time until the sauce is smooth and thick.

DE-GLAZE - To pour liquid (wine, water, stock) in the pan, scraping the bottom to loosen all the particles to use as sauce.

DREDGE - To dip into flour.

DUST - Sprinkle lightly.

ENTREE - A meat or fish served as the main course.

FILLET - Meat or fish without the bones.

FLAMBE - To lighly cover food with spirits, ignite carefully. To add flavor.

FRITTER - Fish, meat, fruit or vegetables coated with a dough and deep fat fried.

JULIENNE - To cut food thin, into matchlike strips.

MARINATE - To add a dressing mixture to food and let stand to season.

MINCE - To cut foods into small cubes.

PUREE - Food boiled until soft and pushed through sieve or food processor.

ROUX - (Baked Flour)
1. Spread flour evenly on sheet pan.
2. Bake at 275° for 2 hours.
3. Store covered.
     For use
1. Melt butter (margarine) until bubbly.
2. Stir in equal amounts of flour.
3. Whip with wire whisk until well mixed.
4. Cook over low heat until the roux has a nutty odor. It should have the consistency of wet sand.
5. Cool and store covered in refrigerator. Used to thicken.

SAUTE - To fry in a small amount of fat.

SCORE - To cut shallow grooves or gashes in the surface of meat.

If you enjoyed
**FAMOUS ADIRONDACK
RESTAURANTS AND RECIPES**
you'll love

TASTES OF THE ADIRONDACK RESTAURANTS

A 248 page New York State Adirondack Mountain cookbook and tour guide including Bed & Breakfast. Enjoy in your own home delectable favorites such as Rumballs Suchard from Rene's in Chestertown, Mexican Salad from Sutton's Cafe in Glens Falls, Capon a la Villa Vespa in Lake Placid, and Sour Cream Apple Pie from the D & H Restaurant in Plattsburgh.

Here is one book you do not want to miss!
HISTORIC AND FAMOUS ALBANY • SARATOGA RESTAURANTS AND RECIPES

This cookbook and travel guide features a collection of recipes from Albany, the capital of New York State and Saratoga Springs, the famous horse racing region. This exciting 224 page cookbook and tour guide offers delectable favorites to enjoy in your own home such as Poppy Seed Bread from Qualters' Pine Hills Restaurant in Albany, Bananas Foster from the Raindancer in Amsterdam, Toasted Coconut Bread from the Caunterbury in Saratoga Springs, Veal and Shrimp from Ridge Terrace in Lake George and Lemon Pie with White Rum from the Shipyard in Latham.

And from the Midwest...

FAMOUS MINNEAPOLIS RESTAURANTS & RECIPES

Takes you on a dining tour of the finest and most fascinating restaurants in Minneapolis. Enjoy in your home culinary specialties such as Lemon Chicken from Leeann Chin Chinese Cuisine, Meat Loaf from the Monte Carlo, Popovers from the Oak Grill, Pears in Port Wine from Mitterhauser La Cuisine and the Duck and Wild Rice Tart from the 510 Restaurant and many more.

You'll like this new book!

FAMOUS VERMONT RESTAURANTS AND RECIPES

This cookbook and travel guide features a collection of Vermont's finest restaurants. The restaurant owners have contributed recipes and food preparations often times using native meats and products. You'll enjoy the Dog Team's Sticky buns, the Trapp Family Lodge's Linzertorte, Tubbs Restaurant's Chocolate Marquise, The Village Country Inn's Two Mushroom soup and the Old Tavern at Grafton's White Chocolate Mousse with Raspberry Sauce, and many more.

212

Here is a Holiday favorite!

A KITCHENFUL OF CHRISTMAS

This book is a delightful collection of Yuletide recipes, poems, stories, and articles. Set to the song, The Twelve Days of Christmas, the book presents recipes for every holiday occasion right down to a Christmas Morning Brunch to celebrate with thee. You'll enjoy recipes such as Grandmother's Eggnog Pie, Candied Sweet Potatoes, Roast Turkey, Baked Broccoli, Mom's Fudge, Fruit Compote, and many more.

BOOK ORDER FORM

Send to: Schildge Publishing Company
P.O. Box 1516
Plattsburgh, New York 12901

_____ copies of **Famous Vermont Restaurants and Recipes** @ $12.95 each $ _____

_____ copies of **Famous Minneapolis Restaurants and Recipes** @ $10.00 each $ _____

_____ copies of **Tastes of the Adirondack Restaurants** @ $12.95 each $ _____

_____ copies of **Famous Adirondack Restaurants & Recipes** @ $12.95 each $ _____

_____ copies of **Historic & Famous Albany • Saratoga Restaurants and Recipes** @ $10.95 each $ _____

_____ copies of **Great Tastes of Vermont Restaurants & Recipes** (not shown) @ $12.95 each $ _____

_____ copies of **A Kitchenful of Christmas** @ $ 9.95 each $ _____

Add postage and handling $1.75 each
Total Enclosed $ _____